THE LIFE AND TIMES
OF
JESUS

© Wyatt North Publishing, LLC 2014

D1603312

About Wyatt North Publishing

Starting out with just one writer, Wyatt North Publishing has expanded to include writers from across the country. Our writers include college professors, religious theologians, and historians.

Wyatt North Publishing provides high quality, perfectly formatted, original books.

Send us an email and we will personally respond within 24 hours! As a boutique publishing company we put our readers first and never respond with canned or automated emails. Send us an email at hello@WyattNorth.com, and you can visit us at www.WyattNorth.com.

About the Author

Michael J. Ruszala holds an M.A. in Theology & Christian Ministry and a B.A. in Philosophy and Theology *summa cum laude* from Franciscan University of Steubenville and is certified as a parish catechetical leader by the Diocese of Buffalo. He is director of faith formation at St. Pius X Catholic Church in Getzville, NY, and an adjunct lecturer in religious studies at Niagara University in Lewiston, NY. Michael is also an active member of the Society of Catholic Social Scientists and serves on the Catechumenate Board and the Faith Formation Assessment Committee for the Diocese of Buffalo. He has been published in several religious journals including the Social Justice Review, the Catholic Social Science Review, and Lay Witness online edition, with articles often touching on contemporary papal teaching. With interests in music, art, tennis, and kayaking, he also enjoys directing the Children's Choir at his parish.

SYRIAN

Caesarea
Philippi

(Herod Antipas)

PHOENICIA

TRACHONITIS

(Philip the Tetrarch)

GALILEE

Capernaum

Bethsaida (?)

BASHAN

MEDITERRANEAN

Cana

SEA

Sep-
phoris

Sea of
Galilee

Nazareth

Caesarea
Maritima

DECAPOLIS

SAMARIA

Sychar

(Herod
Antipas)

(Herod Archelaeus,

River
Jordan

PEREA

later under Roman prefect)

Jericho

Bethany-
over-
Jordan
(?)

Jerusalem

JUDEA

Machaerus

Bethlehem

Wilderness
of Judea

Dead
Sea

To Egypt

IDUMEA

Foreword

To write a book about Jesus is a challenging task; to live a life like Jesus' is more challenging still. Though not primarily a work of theology or of spirituality, this popular history intends to help the words and deeds of Jesus come alive for contemporary readers. In Jesus' day, he was a polarizing figure; one was either for him or against him. Today, even many who are familiar with the story of Jesus are unmoved. There are a number of reasons for this, but one of them is that we have forgotten the history of which Jesus came to be part; and we have also forgotten how we fit in. When God acted in Jesus, he acted in history, and that history came with particular cultures, presuppositions, and memories of its own. Without an understanding of these things, Jesus' polarizing words and deeds become blunted because their backdrop has been removed.

This book is intended for two types of readers. Firstly, it is meant for those who are already familiar with the basic Gospel stories but wish they could enter into them with the eyes of first-century Jews. Secondly, it is intended for those who are not yet familiar with the narrative of Jesus of Nazareth but would like to approach it in an orderly and enjoyable way. It is the first of two books that are planned to approach the life of Jesus of Nazareth from a historical perspective, faithful to the Christian tradition. While the next volume will address more particularly the polarizing nature of Jesus' teachings and, ultimately, his passion, death, and resurrection, this volume covers the story to which Jesus belongs – the world that he entered, his early life, and the beginnings of his ministry. Special attention is given to Palestine under Roman rule, the reign of Herod the Great, the Temple of Jerusalem, the emergence of the canonical Gospels, the figure of John the Baptist, Jesus' proclamation of the Kingdom of God in word and deed, and his teachings in parables and in the Sermon on the Mount.

"One Solitary Life"

He never wrote a book

He never held an office

He never went to college

He never visited a big city

He never travelled more than two hundred miles

From the place where he was born

He did none of the things

Usually associated with greatness

He had no credentials but himself…

Nineteen centuries have come and gone…

All the armies that have ever marched

All the navies that have ever sailed

All the parliaments that have ever sat

All the kings that ever reigned put together

Have not affected the life of mankind on earth

As powerfully as that one solitary life

— by Dr. James Allan

Introduction

By worldly terms, Jesus of Nazareth was born to an insignificant family, raised in an insignificant town; he was a lowly subject in an insignificant province of an empire ruled by cruel men over 1,400 miles across the sea. And yet Jesus of Nazareth did more to change the course of world history than has any other historical figure. Even his enemies did not deny his otherworldly power, and his followers would call him 'Lord' over Lord-Caesar. Though his own kingdom was "not of this world," his own once-persecuted and outlawed followers would overcome the pagan Roman Empire within three centuries, paving the way for an almost thoroughly Christianized Europe for millennia to come. Even today, over 2.1 billion people across every region and continent call themselves Christians, such that nearly one in three persons in the world today consider themselves followers of Christ. And while today's secularized and globalized society has tried to declare its independence from the preacher of Nazareth, it cannot help that it owes much of its own sense of justice, morality, peace, and tolerance to Jesus and his followers. Although many today, looking back at the course of world and European history, assume that society has moved beyond the Way of Christ, G. K. Chesterton reminds us that "Christianity has not been tried and found wanting; it has been found difficult and not tried."

The man called the 'Word' of God by John the Evangelist (in Jn. 1:1) is not known to have ever stained a papyrus with any lines for posterity, yet the books that deal with the implications of what he said and did fill entire libraries. No book has sold more copies or been more widely translated than the Christian Bible, the heart of which is the Gospels of Christ and all of which, Christians believe, is centered on him even in hidden ways. New alphabets have been invented to record his words; countless monks spent their lives writing them and meditating on them; the printing press was invented to distribute them; missionaries have died trying to spread them; nations were founded to live them freely; charities and hospitals were developed to express them more fully. Workmen curse by his name almost without thinking, so ingrained in the western psyche is the all-pervading legacy of that one solitary life lived two thousand years ago.

While today his words are transmitted by satellite, television, social media, books, CDs, and videos, Jesus' contemporaries heard about him first by word of mouth. They heard wondrous things, and troubling things. They were confronted head-on with the identity of this itinerant preacher as the gossip spread through the marketplace, by the well-side, among workers in the field, and from neighbor to neighbor. They had to take a side, and that side brought consequences – as did Jesus' acceptance of certain followers from amongst them.

Zacchaeus was one such man. He was a contrarian of sorts, shrewd enough to find an opportunity to make a handsome living for himself off his nation's unfortunate political situation. His career had led him to become the head tax-collector for the Roman occupiers at Jericho, a city known at the time for its lucrative trade of balsam wood. He collected steep tariffs for the Empire and extorted more for himself on items moving through the city, known even today as the oldest city in the world. Tax collecting was a very profitable business but made him few friends really worth having and left his conscience sick. While his wealth kept accumulating, emotionally, the "wee little man" had hit a low point.

As Zacchaeus glumly went along his way one day, he was caught in a first-century traffic jam because the inhabitants of the city – including many people whom Zacchaeus had tricked and pressured – flooded the streets to see and hear for themselves this Jesus, who had by then made quite a stir touring Galilee to the north and visiting Jerusalem to the west. Perhaps Zacchaeus had heard that Jesus had dared to throw out the moneychangers in the Temple for extortion –

a very similar business to his own yet far more socially tolerated. Perhaps he had heard about Jesus' miracles, which he believed could only come from God. Perhaps he had heard that one of this rabbi's key disciples – Matthew – had been a notorious tax collector in Capernaum in Galilee before hitting the road with Jesus. Perhaps his conscience was pricked. Zacchaeus didn't know exactly who this man was, but he knew he wanted to see for himself. So he found a way around the push and shove of the crowd. He climbed up into a sycamore fig tree and balanced himself on a branch, unperturbed about what people might think of him. Of course, he never did care about that anyway.

To his surprise, the prophet took note of him. "Zacchaeus, come down quickly, for today I must stay at your house" (Lk. 19:5). Zacchaeus was overjoyed that this holy man noticed him, but the crowds were not at all pleased with Jesus' plan to dine with the chief of the local tax collectors. Of all people in town for Jesus to find! But Zacchaeus' heart was changed that day. He even promised to give alms generously as well as to make full restitution even by the strict standards of Jewish religious law: "Behold, half of my possessions, Lord, I shall give to the poor, and if I have extorted anything from anyone I shall repay it four times over." The Bible doesn't tell us what became of Zaccheaus, but we can imagine that from that day, business was never again as usual for Zaccheaus; and his relationships with the Romans, with the tax collectors, with the townspeople, and with his own carefully procured wealth were forever altered. There were consequences for his choice, and he could never look back. Yet he found something more valuable than all the silver, gold, and trade-portions that he had so shrewdly been collecting.

In the same way, we too are confronted by the person of Jesus. Many people know about Jesus, yet few truly know him. The common people of Judea, Galilee, Samaria, and the regions neighboring greater Palestine knew him in a way that we never can. In some ways we have an advantage over them because of the two-thousand-year tradition of the Church. For many of them, their perspective of him was raw and mostly un-reflected. Jesus asked his disciples what the people thought of him, as to his identity. They replied, "Some say John the Baptist, others Elijah, still others Jeremiah or one of the prophets" (Mt. 16:14). While people still have many false opinions about Jesus, no one would say those things today. But because of the tradition of the Church, we long for what these people had – yet did not know that they had. While many of those people did not understand him, for others the experience of Jesus of Nazareth was sufficient cause to endure social persecution, time in prison, torture, and execution.

This book aims to give us a historical glimpse into the first-century experience of Jesus of Nazareth. It will treat in basic terms the religious, political, and cultural situation that set the stage for what St. Paul calls the "fullness of time" (Gal. 4:4). It wasn't a glamorous time. It was more the kind of time that most of us are grateful we don't have to endure. But this book will prepare us to take our place within the crowd, to hear Jesus preach and see him perform mighty deeds, when we open up the Gospels for ourselves. While no one today would say that Jesus is John the Baptist, Elijah, or Jeremiah, we will see for ourselves if we agree with our own contemporaries that Jesus of Nazareth was simply a great man, a noble teacher, a religious founder, and an unfortunate martyr. Or perhaps we agree with the sour-faced scholars who tell us that Jesus of Nazareth was a failed messiah who never intended to found a religion and that the religion bearing his name has done little to further the material progress of the world.

Pope Benedict XVI reflects in *Jesus of Nazareth*, "What did Jesus actually bring, if not world peace, universal prosperity, and a better world? What has he brought? The answer is very simple: God. He has brought God. He has brought the God who formerly unveiled his countenance gradually, first to Abraham, then to Moses and the Prophets…. He has brought God, and now we know his face, now we can call upon him. Now we know the path that we human beings have to take in this world. Jesus has brought God and with God the truth about our origin and destiny: faith, hope, and love."

The Story of a People

Open to the beginning of the New Testament and the genealogy of Jesus is what you will find. Most skip over it while others bravely plough their way through it. But much like Matthew, the writer of the first Gospel, I too feel the need to express before anything else that the story of Jesus does not begin with Jesus of Nazareth. A great history is presupposed – a history that his fellow countrymen would have known as well as we know the names of our own grandparents. The only question is: how far back should we go? For Matthew, the answer was to go back to Abraham, the ancient father of the Jewish people, whom God had called out of the city of Ur in Mesopotamia in a journey of faith to the land of Canaan, later called Palestine. For Luke the Evangelist, the answer was Adam, the father of the human race, emphasizing that Jesus came for all peoples.

Very basically, the history presupposed is that of God's intervention in human affairs, particularly those of the Chosen People, the Children of Israel. The Bible tells us that God spoke to Abraham, bringing him into a covenant with God alone as God, as opposed to the many false gods of his ancestors. As God promised, he made Abraham into a vast people, and that people was later liberated from slavery in Egypt by Moses. The Bible tells us that God spoke to Moses and made a covenant with Moses. And through Moses, God made the people a nation, replete with laws to govern them. Then there was David, the greatest king of Israel, a man "after God's own heart." And the Bible tells us that God spoke to David and made a covenant with him, promising that his kingdom would last forever and even that his son would be God's son. But no sooner had David died than the kingdom was severed in two by a rivalry, never to rise again to the full glory it had known under David. The history of the kings of Israel and Judah became a history of turning away from God and of God punishing the kingdoms for their sins. First the Northern Kingdom was conquered, and the survivors were carried off by the Assyrians in the eighth century BC under King Sennacherib. Then, in the sixth century BC, the Kingdom of Judah to the south was conquered by the Babylonians under King Nebuchadnezzar; and the survivors were marched off to Babylon in chains. Then came Jesus, whom the Bible calls the "Word" of God made flesh (Jn. 1) – Jesus, who told Pilate before his execution, "my kingdom is not of this world."

But before Jesus, there came the Persians, then the Greeks, and then the Romans. In 538 BC, the Persians under King Cyrus conquered the Babylonians and allowed the Hebrew captives to return to their homeland and rebuild their Temple in Jerusalem, which King Solomon, the son of David, had first constructed. The Persians held control of Palestine for centuries, but the Jews were fairly content to have the Persians for their rulers since they were better than the alternatives. Then, in 332 BC, Alexander the Great took control of Palestine from the Persians. His reign was vast but short lived. Having died at the age of 33, his empire was given to his heirs and divided into four kingdoms. The Seleucid kingdom to the north and the Ptolemaic kingdom, based in Egypt to the south, would vie between themselves for control of Palestine. Judas Maccabaeus and his brothers led a bloody revolt in the mid-second century BC against Palestine's Seleucid rulers, who were trying to force the Jews to violate Jewish religious laws and customs. Remarkably, the Maccabees did gain independence. Ultimately the Jews assented to become a client kingdom under the Seleucids, granted that they could practice their religion in peace and manage their own affairs. Springing from Jonathan, the brother of Judas Maccabeus, the Jewish Hasmonean dynasty ruled over this semi-independent kingdom in Palestine from 140 to 110 BC, then existing as a fully independent kingdom from 110 to 63 BC.

During the revolt, the Maccabees had made an alliance with the Roman Republic. But as the Republic morphed into the greatest empire the western world has ever known,

Palestine, too, fell prey to its ambitions. Taking advantage of a civil war in the Hasmonean kingdom, Pompey conquered Jerusalem in 63 BC, establishing the Roman province of Judea. He killed some 12,000 Jews and desecrated the Temple. When it came to the actual practice of the Jewish religion, however, Pompey learned from his Greek predecessors not to interfere too much – a precedent that would last for the remaining centuries of Roman rule. But the Romans had plenty of areas other than religion in which to impose their power through fear and cruelty. Burdensome taxes were levied to pay for the expanding Roman Empire. The commentator Vermont Royester, as quoted by O'Reilly and Dugard, wrote of the Romans "There was enslavement of men whose tribes came not from Rome…. And most of all, there was contempt for human life. What, to the strong, was one man more or less in a crowded world?" The slaughter by Pompey was nothing compared to the Roman response to the revolt in Judea, culminating in AD 70, in which around one million Jews according to Josephus' estimate lost their lives. Anyone fleeing Jerusalem during the siege was crucified – hundreds every day, such that the first-century Judeo-Roman historian Flavius Josephus recounts that there were not enough crosses for the bodies.

Crucifixion was not invented by the Romans, but it was elaborated sadistically by them. Crucifixion had been used by the Seleucids in Palestine before the Romans, and was used by other powers in the ancient world. The Romans used it as an extreme deterrent and sign of contempt for conquered peoples and for slaves. In fact, the ancient writer Valerius Maximus called it the 'slave's punishment.' Crucifixion was not mentioned in polite Roman society, but soldiers experimented with various forms as a kind of cruel sport. This long and drawn-out form of execution was deplorably common for non-citizens and slaves, and gibbets for crucifixion were placed outside of major cities such as Jerusalem. It struck shame and dread into the hearts of all, lest anyone dare defy the powers that be. Bloody crucifixes were a common sight in the days of Christ, though the Romans did not hesitate to use their many other dreadful ways of punishing or executing insubordinate provincials as well. But not only did the Jews have the Romans to deal with, they were also under the iron hand of Herod the Great, who called himself the 'King of the Jews.'

The Reign of Herod the Great

The Gospel of Matthew tells us about the enraged despot who ordered all the baby boys in Bethlehem slaughtered to prevent the rise of the new "king of the Jews" sought by the magi (Mt. 2:1). This ruler was the iconic and infamous Herod the Great, who ruled from 37 BC to 4 BC, seizing power from the Hasmoneans who had been allowed to continue as client kings under the Romans. Herod was the son of Antipater the Idumaean, an Edomite from south of Palestine who became a convert to Judaism. Antipater had been a high-ranking official in the semi-independent Hasmonean kingdom before the Romans, but he won favor with Julius Caesar by offering him valuable services when the latter was fleeing from Pompey. Julius Caesar made Antipater chief minister of Judea. After his death, his son Herod went to Rome to petition for himself to be declared 'King of the Jews.' His wish was granted by the Senate. Herod allied with Mark Antony, but after the general's defeat, Herod shrewdly sought to win favor with Antony's rival, Caesar Augustus, who confirmed his title.

Herod grew up in opulence and learned the cunning of his father. He learned from him not to bite the hand that feeds you, at least until a better or more powerful hand comes around. Herod had to appease the Romans to avoid being removed from higher up, and he had to placate the people to avoid being overthrown. And his courtiers and others he came across had to please him and tend to his whims or else they would be immediately seized by the guards and killed by any means – except crucifixion, which was reserved by the Romans alone. The Jews were wise to Herod's allegiances, the most important of which was to himself.

Though a convert to Judaism to please the Jews, Herod's actions were far from obedient to the Law of the Lord. Herod's ambitions were boundless, as was his fear of any threats to his power, which the Bible describes in the account of his reaction to the birth of a new 'King of the Jews.' The Jews did not accept Herod because he was not of Davidic lineage, or of any noble lineage for that matter, and he was not a Jew by blood. When he became king, he cast off his pagan wife Doris and their son and arranged for marriage to the beautiful young Jewish Hasmonean princess Mariamne I, claiming her lineage as his own. In fact, he even had all of the written Davidic genealogies that he could find destroyed to hide his own, lower lineage – though not even the Hasmoneans were in the line of David. He loved Mariamne passionately, even though she despised him and, as Josephus tells us, with cause. Herod had much of her family, members of the Hasmonean line, killed, including Mariamne's father and her brother, the high priest

Aristobulus III, who died in a staged drowning accident. As the queen discovered, Herod also gave orders that Mariamne should not be allowed to live past his own death. Josephus tells us that Herod later had Mariamne executed, falsely charged by Herod's sister Salome, an enemy of Mariamne, with infidelity, but that he regretted the sentence after his rage subsided. Other sources tell us that the charge stemmed from a plot to poison Herod. Herod nearly went mad after having Mariamne killed. In fact, Herod is said to have had her body preserved in honey for seven years and to have continued to have relations with her. In fact, the Talmud refers to such an act as 'the deed of Herod.' He also had a tower he built on the wall of Jerusalem named after her. Herod had many wives later on, and a number of divorces. He had three of his own elder sons executed for treason. In addition to being known as a treacherous man, Herod angered the Jews by introducing circuses in honor of the emperor and by building temples to pagan gods.

Herod, who had himself styled 'the Great,' was nonetheless effective at getting things done in Judea. His building projects were of such grand scale that if one could have seen them from space, they probably would have been the most visible manmade structures in the region. These projects were intended to secure unending fame for himself and esteem from his subjects. He built a great port on the Mediterranean at Caesarea Maritima. He also poured resources into the construction of key cities in Galilee, such as Sypphoris, which was not far from Jesus' hometown of Nazareth; and he built several impressive castles for himself at Masada, Caesarea, and Tiberias. His most famous project was the grand renovation and vast expansion of the Temple at Jerusalem, which became known as Herod's Temple. Herod's projects were undoubtedly expensive, so he laid backbreaking taxes on the populace on top of the Roman taxes, leading to more dissatisfaction among the people. Some were reduced to slavery or prostitution over their inability to pay. Still, the projects ensured much opportunity for employment. Perhaps Joseph, the foster father of Jesus, who was a builder, received his employment in the construction of Herod's cities in Galilee.

Jesus was born in Bethlehem just a short time before the old, sick, but still quick-tempered king died in 4 BC. If "all Jerusalem" (Mt. 2:3) was indeed troubled over there being a new 'King of the Jews,' it was most likely because of there being more trouble from Herod. The magi, perhaps oriental astrologers who discovered the new king's star, were warned in a dream not to believe Herod's story about wanting to know where the child was to give him homage, so they avoided Herod during their return home. After hearing from the scribes and chief priests that Bethlehem was the prophesied birthplace of the new king, Herod sent out soldiers to slaughter all of the male children in Bethlehem under the age of two. While the surviving historical record does not provide evidence of this massacre of innocents, Bethlehem was only a small and insignificant town, and we do know from history that Herod was not the type to balk at such an act.

Warned in a dream, Joseph escaped to Egypt with Mary and the child Jesus. They would not have had long to wait before the end of Herod's long reign – perhaps a year or two. Herod designated no clear heir to his throne, so three of his remaining sons petitioned Rome for their father's kingdom after his death in 4 BC. So Caesar Augustus split the kingdom and gave a portion to each of them, though he withheld the title of 'king' from them. This arrangement became known as the 'tetrarchy,' a name that implies a division of rule into quarters, even though there were only three rulers. This was because Herod Archelaus, called 'ethnarch' in the Gospels, ruled over half, and Herod Antipas and Herod Philip, both 'tetrarchs,' ruled over the remaining quarters.

The ethnarch Herod Archelaus ruled over the peoples of Judea, Samaria, and Idumea. Archelaus was notorious for his cruelty, and the Bible tells us that Joseph's fear of him is the reason the family returned to Nazareth rather than stopping again in his hometown of Bethlehem (Mt. 2:22). Archelaus massacred thousands of Jews in Jerusalem who had protested his policies. In fact, he was deposed by Caesar Augustus in AD 6 on account of the reports of his cruelty. Nazareth was under the rule of Herod Antipas, who controlled Galilee and Perea. Years later, Herod Antipas would have John the Baptist killed and would hear the case against Jesus before returning him to Pilate. Philip the Tetrarch ruled the Transjordan to the east of the Sea of Galilee. Philip himself did not make much trouble. But notably, his brother Herod Antipas in Galilee took and married Philip's wife Herodias, which created the scandal condemned by the John the Baptist (Mk. 6:20-28). Furthermore, it was Herodias' daughter Salome who danced before Herod Antipas, eliciting his offer of anything "even to half of my kingdom." The girl's mother Herodias had her ask for the head of John the Baptist even though he was a prophet respected by most of the people.

The Temple: The Center of the Jewish World

The Gospels speak of Jesus' disciples gazing in astonishment at the glory of the massive walled edifice on the Temple Mount in Mark 13:1 when they went up to the holy city of Jerusalem. Their view from the Mount of Olives across the Kidron Valley to Herod's Temple would have been a sight to behold; they would have seen the towering, sparkling sanctuary surrounded by a beautiful expanse of giant blocks of stone and jutting high over nearly the whole perimeter of the Temple Mount. That holy plateau, also called Mount Zion or Mount Moriah, is the one on which Abraham had been willing to sacrifice his son Isaac before being stopped by an angel. There God had ordered his Temple to be built, and King Solomon had overseen its first construction.

As for any Jew, the Temple would be important in the life of Jesus. Every devout Jewish man was obligated to "go up" to the Temple, on the "Mountain of the Lord," every year for Passover, and also for the Feast of Pentecost and Tabernacles. During Passover, each family (or groups of families) would offer a lamb, often purchased at the Temple itself, for the priests in the Temple to sacrifice on the 14th of Nisan. Then the family would have to eat the meat completely by the night of the following day to commemorate God's deliverance of the people from Egypt. It was during this sacrifice that the Gospel of John places the death of Jesus on the cross (Jn. 19:14). The Temple is also where Jesus was presented according to Jewish law, 40 days after his birth, with his parents offering the poor person's sacrifice of two turtle doves purchased at the Temple rather than the lamb that only the rich could afford. It was also where he "got lost" among the elders at the age of twelve and where he preached bold sermons on numerous occasions as a man. The Temple also had unique significance for Jesus. For him singularly it was "my Father's house" (Lk. 2:49). Christ even identified his own body, the dwelling place of God, with the Temple; when standing in the Temple courtyard he said, "Destroy this temple and in three days I will raise it up" (Jn. 2:19).

On the southern end of the Temple and rising high over the Kidron Valley was the roofed colonnade of Solomon's Portico, which survived from Solomon's original Temple. It was there that Jesus told the Jews, "The Father and I are one" (Jn. 10:30). The Temple was modeled after the tent of the Tabernacle, which God had instructed Moses to set up such that the outer areas had lesser degrees of holiness and were more common while the inner areas were holier and more exclusive. First, in the Temple, there was the large open-air Court of the Gentiles, which was the place of much talking, buying, and selling. This is where Jesus overturned the tables of the moneychangers. Then, in a more enclosed area, was the Court of Women. A ways before, the entrance bore a placard that indicated that any Gentile who dared pass any further would be killed instantly. Next was the Court of the Israelites, in which only adult Israelite men could enter, before the Court of the Priests. Finally, at the center was the nine-story sanctuary with its gilded façade enclosing the Holy of Holies. At the sanctuary, priests would offer sacrifices to the Lord, including the morning sacrifice and the evening sacrifice each day. Only the high priest could enter the Holy of Holies, the innermost part of the sanctuary, and even he could only do so once a year. It was intended to house the Ark of the Covenant, but now it was empty since the Ark of the Covenant had long been lost to Israel's enemies and its location is unknown to this day. It was at the Holy of Holies that, the Gospels tell us, the massive veil enclosing the Holy of Holies was mysteriously torn in two from top to bottom after the death of Christ (Mt. 27:51).

Priests offering sacrifices in the Temple were called into service from those men of age in the tribe of Levi, to whom God had given the priesthood. The high priest, of whom there was only one at a time, was to be a Levite descended from Aaron. The Hasmonean kings took the high priesthood for themselves since their forefather Jonathan, the brother of Judas Maccabeus, had been named high priest in 153 BC after the Jews had gained their independence. Still, they had to compete with other families for the claim to rightful high priesthood since Jonathan did not come from the same line as his predecessors. During the reign of Herod the Great, he at first kept the Hasmoneans as the high priests. But after he had finished killing off the Hasmoneans as threats to his throne, he simply appointed different men from the line of Aaron to serve as high priest each year. As high priests, these men would ritually prepare and separate themselves for one week before entering the Holy of Holies on the Day of Atonement one time only in their lives, wearing a blue garment, a turban covering their head, and twelve jewels above their waist to represent the twelve tribes of Israel. Once they had finished their term, these men joined an elite council of high priests with special religious influence. These were likely the 'chief priests' frequently referenced in the Gospels.

For Christians, the mysterious tearing of the sanctuary veil meant that, as the writer of the Letter to the Hebrews says, "Christ came as high priest … passing through the greater and more perfect tabernacle not made by hands" (Heb. 9:11). He sees Jesus as solving – or, shall we say, fulfilling – the problem that the high priesthood had become by offering a perfect and spiritual sacrifice to God on the cross "once for all" (Heb. 10:8).

By the time Jesus visited the Temple, the Gospels tell us, it had been under construction for 46 years (Jn. 2:20). Herod, however, angered the Pharisees by having a golden eagle, a symbol of the Roman Empire, placed over the entrance to the Temple. The Pharisees saw this as an idolatrous symbol and an abomination. In response to his disciples' astonishment at the grandness of the Temple, Jesus prophesied, "Do you see these great buildings? There will not be one stone left upon another that will not be thrown down" (Mk. 13:2). The 'Eagle' of Rome would swoop down in 70 AD and destroy the Temple in response to a popular revolt, even using Jewish galley slaves to do the task for them. Today, the great stones and the craters that they made in the earth below remain immortalized as some of the few remnants from the Temple. Citing the prophets, Jesus prophesied of the destruction of the Temple: "the sun will be darkened, and the moon will not give its light, and the stars will be falling from the sky, and the powers in the heavens will be shaken" (Mk. 13:24-25). For the first-century Jews, the end of the Temple was the end of their world in religious, political, and social terms. Life would never be the same, even to the present day.

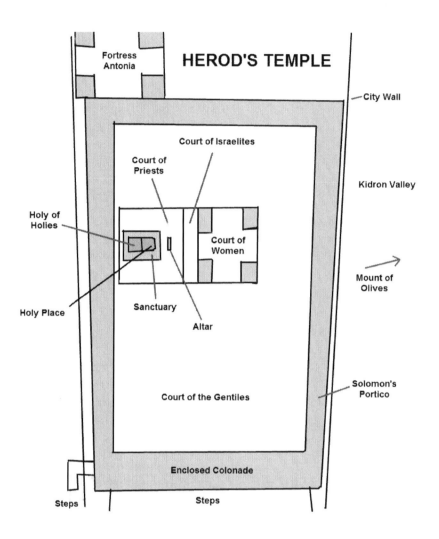

Who's Who in First Century Palestine

Just beyond the Temple to the north, but bordering its walls, was the Fortress Antonia with its four massive turrets, even higher than the sanctuary of the Temple. Built by Herod, it was a stronghold of Roman military power. The man in charge of the Roman armies in the region was Pontius Pilate. A stone inscription discovered in 1961 names Pontius Pilate as prefect, a military position he held from AD 26 to AD 36. Later, the same position was called 'procurator.' He would have had 500 to 1,000 soldiers under him to maintain the occupation in Palestine, and he was also responsible for Roman taxation. Herod provided the living accommodations for both Pilate and his wife, since the law changed in AD 21 to allow wives to accompany their husbands who held such positions abroad.

Born in central Italy, Pilate was no friend of the Jews. Josephus records that Pilate was prone to rage and was very brutal to the Jews and callous to their religious sensitivities. Luke 13:1 refers to those "Galileans whose blood Pilate had mingled with the blood of their sacrifices." Also, knowing that the Jews abhorred graven images (as forbidden in the Ten Commandments), Pilate contemptuously marched into Jerusalem with standard banners bearing the face of the divine Caesar. Even the Herodians, not themselves known for their humanitarian dispositions, decried his cruelty towards the Jews. The Jews vehemently protested Pilate's iron governance, and ultimately Caesar Tiberius called him back to Rome in AD 36 on reports that he had conducted a massacre in Samaria. Pilate told Jesus, "I have power to release you and I have the power to crucify you" (Jn. 19:10). This was ordinarily a power that Pilate took quite lightly.

The chambers of the Temple were likely the venue for the Sanhedrin, the religious, political, and legal authority of the Jews. In the time of Christ, it probably consisted of 71 members, including both Pharisees and Sadducees, who sat in a semicircle when in session with two scribes in front to keep records. The high priest presided over its meetings. The membership of the Sanhedrin comprised three groups: the chief priests, a group of men who had at one point been high priest; scribes, whose profession we will explain below; and elders, who were the other distinguished appointees, whether priestly or lay. The Sanhedrin's roots went back to the governing body that had been created by the governor Zerbubbabel after the Jews had returned to Jerusalem from the Exile in Babylon. This ruling body used to decide cases of life or death, but the authority to administer capital punishment was removed by the Romans in AD 6 with the appointment of the first Roman prefect of Judea. This is why the Sanhedrin sent Jesus to Pilate for a sentence of death (Jn.

18:31). Still, the Sanhedrin sometimes administered the death penalty in between the prefects' appointments.

Josephus lists three "philosophical sects among the Jews," which were also important in the life of Jesus (JW 2.8.2). These were the Pharisees and Sadducees, who also figure prominently in conflict with Jesus in the Gospels, and the Essenes, who are not directly referenced in the New Testament but had many interesting similarities to the Christianity that would soon emerge. Most ordinary Jews, however, did not belong to any of these groups.

The Pharisees, according to Josephus, "appear more religious than others, and seem to interpret the laws more accurately" (JW 1.5.2). It seems the Pharisees could be traced back at least to the period after the Maccabean revolt, and they are considered highly influential in the development of rabbinic literature – such as the Talmud, a large collection of instructions on the Torah, and the Mishnah, a collection of opinions on matters of law. These were written down in the centuries following Christ and provided much guidance for the practice of Judaism in the Diaspora after the Temple was destroyed in AD 70. The Pharisees believed that the soul survives death, that the just will receive the resurrection of the body, and that God is involved in the world through providence in human affairs. Josephus tells us that the Pharisees received much respect from ordinary Jews, but that they also often overstepped their bounds by getting excessively entangled in the politics of the Hasmoneans and Herodians.

A number of Pharisees invited Jesus over for dinner, and a small number became followers of the Way, though they wanted to retain the strict practice of the Law of Moses. The nature of this Law, which came from Moses in the Torah, was moral, civil, and ceremonial, with the latter aspect having much to do with physical purification. Mark explains examples of these customs to the Gentile readers of his Gospel: "For the Pharisees and, in fact, all Jews, do not eat without carefully washing their hands, keeping the tradition of the elders. And on coming from the marketplace they do not eat without purifying themselves. And there are many other things that they have traditionally observed, the purification of cups and jugs and kettles [and beds]" (Mk. 7:3-4). Although many of these rules were added as extensions to Moses' laws by the Pharisees and the rabbis, Christians believe that Moses' ceremonial laws serve to point to Christ and have been fulfilled by his Law – that, for example, the ritual physical purification pointed to cleanness of soul.

Jesus says in the Gospels, "The scribes and the Pharisees have taken their seat on the chair of Moses. Therefore, do and observe all things whatsoever they tell you, but do not follow their example. For they preach but they do not practice. They tie up heavy burdens [hard to carry] and lay them on people's shoulders, but they will not lift a finger to move them" (Mt. 23:2-4). Thus Jesus accepted the authority of the Pharisees while condemning their moral disposition. The scribes were members of an esteemed profession, although it is likely that many of them at the time of Christ were of the party of the Pharisees. Recording and copying the history and laws of Judaism, the scribes themselves became experts. In Jesus' day, these scholarly scribes filled a number of prestigious functions. They preserved the documents of the Law; they expounded on the Law and set practical guidelines for living it; they served as teachers of pupils in the Temple; they heard legal cases; and they were esteemed for their preaching in the synagogues, although that function was open to any Jewish adult male.

The party of the Pharisees is often contrasted with that of the Sadducees, who arose near the same point in history. The Sadducees did not believe that the soul survives death or that there would be a resurrection of the dead. Further, they only accepted the Torah, the first five books of the

Bible, and did not believe that God is providentially interested in the affairs of the world. In fact, St. Paul took advantage of these differences to provoke an argument between the two sects and divert attention from himself in his hearing before the Sanhedrin (Acts 23:6). On these points, Jesus was actually closer to the Pharisees. The Sadducees were not nearly as influential in the history of Judaism as the Pharisees, and Josephus tells us that they were a cantankerous lot. Many scholars believe that the Sadducees tended to be connected with priestly families while the Pharisees were not. Also, it was the Sadducees who ultimately effected Jesus' demise in Jerusalem.

The Essenes were another sect of the Jews. They placed their trust in a mysterious 'Teacher of Righteousness' who was said to be a high priest before Jonathan, the brother of Judas Maccabees, and who would come again to illuminate the truth and set all aright. The Essenes practiced celibacy, lived in community, had much fraternal love for one another, practiced an austere lifestyle, held all things in common, said grace before meals, took ritual baths each day, and required an extended period of initiation for newcomers. While the most famous Essene community was the one at the excavation site at Qumran in the desert, the site of the discovery of the Dead Sea Scrolls in a cave in the mid-twentieth century, Josephus tells us that the Essenes had communities all throughout Palestine and admitted both men and women. Some speculate that John the Baptist may have lived among the Essenes prior to his ministry of preaching and baptism.

Expectations for the Messiah

The title 'Christ' means 'Anointed One.' All the canonical Gospels apply this title to Jesus, and St. Paul begins referring to 'Christ Jesus' throughout his epistles. It is the Greek equivalent of the Hebrew word 'Messiah.' Based on the prophecies of the Hebrew Scriptures, the Jews had long awaited this leader whom God would send his people. This term was used in the Hebrew Scriptures to refer to kings established by God, especially Davidic kings. In Daniel 9:25, it refers directly to the one to come at the end of the age who will make all things right. But it seems that the word 'Messiah' was not completely reserved for the latter meaning in the Jewish world and among the rabbis until after the destruction of the Temple in AD 70, one generation after the death of Jesus. The destruction of the Temple brought new urgency to this hope, but the prophecies and the hope had been known for thousands of years – such that "a shoot shall sprout from the stump of Jesse," the father of King David (Is. 11:1).

The zealots sought to bring about the prophesies of the Messiah, especially in their political aspects. While Josephus, who switched his allegiances to the Roman Empire by the time of his writing, does not list them among the philosophical sects of Judaism, he records the actions of these men, who were a thorn in the side of the establishment. They were freedom fighters, 'social bandits,' guerilla warriors, and, in some cases, messiah-claimants. In fact, one of Jesus' apostles – Simon the Zealot – had been part of these movements before following Jesus. Indeed, some modern scholars have famously but wrongly associated Jesus himself, who instead taught that "all who take the sword will perish by the sword" (Mt. 26:52), with the movement of the zealots, claiming him to be another failed messiah.

While the Romans granted the Jews basic freedom to worship, social unrest brewed in Palestine under Roman rule. Roman occupation meant all-out exploitation of the people and their resources for the interests of Rome. Looking at models of first-century Jerusalem, grandly renovated by Herod the Great, we see that some neighborhoods were quite well-off. Others were not, with the peasants forced to live in little hovels within the walled limits of the city. Under Roman rule, this divide between the rich and poor grew. The rich, like Zachaeus the tax collector or King Herod at the extreme, were the ones who generally found a way to make the most of Roman occupation and get along with their overlords. Even the Pharisees, while not ultimately happy with Roman occupation, came to know their place comfortably within Roman rule and not to bite the hand that fed them. The only relationship the poor had with the Romans was one of fear and dread.

'Social bandits' roamed about, raiding and otherwise undermining the establishment. They would attack the interests of Herod and of the Romans and terrorize any of the wealthy who were friendly with the establishment. Herod the Great launched several military operations to try to wipe them out. Meanwhile the poor cheered them on, and one group of bandits and zealots would ally with other groups to bring about greater cover for themselves and more trouble for the rulers. Some believe that the two men crucified with Jesus may not have been common thieves but rather were 'social bandits' of this type. The word used in Mark 15:27 to describe them could be translated as 'thieves,' 'robbers,' or 'brigands.'

Josephus tells us about a number of zealots who claimed to be the Messiah. All of these met a violent end. Several peasant zealots emerged to make themselves King of the Jews in place of Herod Archelaus prior to his deposal in AD 6. The most significant zealot-messiah was Simon bar Giora, who rose up in AD 66. He raised an army and briefly gained control of Jerusalem and parts of Judea and Idumea. His reign provoked the infamous destruction of Jerusalem by the

Romans under Titus in AD 70, which resulted in the loss of the Temple and one million Jewish lives. As Titus breached the walls of Jerusalem, Simon fled into underground passageways, but he ran out of supplies. Starving, he dug his way out and emerged on the newly leveled Temple Mount, dressed in the purple garb of the King of the Jews. Captured by the Romans, he was paraded in chains triumphantly around Rome before being thrown to his death off the Tarpeian Rock near the Temple of Jupiter. Meanwhile in AD 73, Jewish forces at Herod's old fortress Masada, in the desert bordering the Dead Sea, committed mass suicide to avoid total defeat and capture by the approaching Romans, who had successfully set up siege machines against the high and massive stronghold. Even after all this, the Jews still did not give up their quest for independence. Another failed messiah, supported by a leading rabbi, was Simon ben Kosiba, who emerged in AD 132. He took control of Jerusalem and even minted his own coins, dated "Year 1 of the liberation of Israel." He was driven from Jerusalem by the Romans, and he and his men were forced into a mass suicide much like that at Masada years before.

Josephus, a Romanized Jew, distanced himself from the zealots and insisted that they were only a radical segment of the Jewish population. With the exception of those times that the zealots had provoked all-out war for life or death with the Romans, the zealots did not represent the interests of most Jews. The Gospels, in fact, picture the Pharisees showing much concern for preserving the status quo with the Romans. The Pharisees of the Sanhedrin gave this counsel about Jesus: "If we leave him alone, all will believe in him, and the Romans will come and take away both our land and our nation" (Jn. 11:38).

As biblical scholar Brant Pitre reminds us, the first-century Jews in general were not only looking for the Messiah to free them from the Romans and the Herodians. For example, while the Jews considered it blasphemous to compare any ordinary prophet to Moses since Moses had seen God and spoken with him as a friend, Moses foretold that someday a "prophet like me" would arise (Deut. 18:15). God had promised to David that his son would be God's son and that he would reign on the throne forever (2 Sam. 7:11-17). Through him, God would establish a new covenant, written on the hearts of his people (Jer. 31:31-34). And he would offer acceptable sacrifice to God, unlike the previous sacrifices, which did not please God (Mal. 3:1-4). While the shepherds of Israel looked to themselves and not their sheep, God himself would shepherd his people and raise up a Davidic ruler to care for them (Ezek. 34:23). Dozens of other passages further promise a spectacular leader sent by God.

In addition to the hope for a new covenant, there was also the hope for a new exodus surpassing the one by which Moses had led the people out from slavery in Egypt. There was also hope for a new Temple – one whose Holy of Holies would not be empty like in Herod's Temple and one that would please God by its sacrifices. Wholeness would also come to the people, especially the poor and needy, as Isaiah had prophesied: "Then the eyes of the blind shall see, and the ears of the deaf be opened; Then the lame shall leap like a stag, and the mute tongue sing for joy" (Is. 35:5-6).

This anointed leader who "comes in the name of the LORD" (Ps. 118:26) would be a priest to offer fitting sacrifice, a prophet to reveal God to the people in a way that surpassed even Moses, and a king who would lead the people forever as God himself would do. It is this broader and deeper hope for a 'Christ' that the Gospels draw from and interpret. In light of this hope of Jesus as Christ, even Simon the Zealot would abandon his sword and political aspirations.

The Historical Record on Jesus

It was part of the Soviet curriculum for schoolchildren to learn that 'Jesus of Nazareth' was not a historical figure at all but was instead invented by the early Christians for their own purposes. This view, prejudiced by ideology, is now clearly known to be untenable. Besides the Christian Gospels, there are multiple references to Jesus in first-century Jewish and Roman documents. There are many references in the New Testament that are deeply embedded in history, intertwined with the nitty-gritty of real life people, places, and things in first-century Palestine. Furthermore, Jesus' disciples preferred to face death rather than deny their Lord. Only one of Jesus' Twelve Apostles was spared martyrdom; the Apostle John is believed to have ended his days in exile on the island of Patmos.

Josephus himself testifies to the historicity of Jesus. He writes, "Now there was about this time Jesus, a wise man, if it be lawful to call him a man; for he was a doer of wonderful works, a teacher of such men as receive the truth with pleasure. He drew over to him both many of the Jews and many of the Gentiles. He was [the] Christ. And when Pilate, at the suggestion of the principal men amongst us, had condemned him to the cross, those that loved him at the first did not forsake him; for he appeared to them alive again the third day; as the divine prophets had foretold these and ten thousand other wonderful things concerning him. And the tribe of Christians, so named from him, are not extinct at this day" (Ant. 18.3.3). It seems that the phrase "He was [the] Christ" was added by later copyists, however.

Pliny the Younger, the Roman governor of Pontus in Asia Minor, wrote to the Emperor Trajan around AD 110 to seek advice for what to do with the followers of Christ who refused to burn incense to the emperor. He said that officials had handed over Christians to him but that he only gathered from the accusers that "they were accustomed to meet on a fixed day before dawn and sing responsively a hymn to Christ as to a god, and to bind themselves by oath, not to some crime, but not to commit fraud, theft, or adultery, not falsify their trust, nor to refuse to return a trust when called upon to do so." He thought that besides insubordination to his demands, their greatest guilt was subscribing to "depraved, excessive superstition." Trajan responded that obstinate Christians should be punished, but they should not be sought out.

The Roman historian Suetonius wrote in his *Lives of the Twelve Caesars* in AD 121 about the Emperor Claudius, who reigned only a few years after the death of Jesus, from AD 41 to AD 54: "He banished from Rome all the Jews, who were continually making disturbances at the instigation of one Chrestos." Most likely Suetonius mistook 'Christos,' the title that Christians applied to Jesus, for the common name 'Chrestos.' In fact, Acts 18:1-4 records this same expulsion of the Jews from Rome by Claudius.

The Roman historian Tacitus (AD 56 - ca. 117) also testifies to the early followers of Christ in Rome and to the historicity of Christ himself. The Emperor Nero, who ruled from AD 54 to AD 68, set fire to the city of Rome with the intention of building a new city. This, of course, greatly angered the citizens, whose losses in the fire were very great. When they began to suspect the emperor of setting the fire, Tacitus reports that Nero shifted the blame to the Christians. Nero then hunted down the Christians and devised many cruel deaths for them. Tacitus further reports of Christ himself: "Christus, from whom the name had its origin, suffered the extreme penalty during the reign of Tiberius at the hands of one of our procurators, Pontius Pilatus, and a most mischievous superstition, thus checked for the moment, again broke out not only in Judaea, the first source of the evil, but even in Rome, where all things hideous and shameful from every part of the world find their centre and become popular."

References to Christ and the early Christians also dot the Jewish rabbinic literature, such as the Mishnah and the Talmud. Mentioning Christ by name, however, was not allowed, and Christianity was seen as a pernicious threat. The crime of believing in Jesus as Christ was referred to as 'Minuth.' Jesus himself was referred to by pejorative nicknames. Howard Clark Kee writes in *What Can We Know About Jesus?*, "In some passages of this Jewish material, he is called 'Ben Stada,' 'Ben Pandira,' or 'Ben Panthera,' implying that he is the illegitimate son (Ben, in Hebrew) of a soldier or some other unworthy person. Similarly, his mother is pictured as disreputable." Kee also quotes Joseph Klausner, a Jewish scholar, in affirming that the historical data about Jesus from the rabbinic literature is mostly consistent with the Gospels except on the number of his inner circle: "There are reliable statements to the effect that his name was Yeshu'a of Nazareth; that he 'practiced sorcery' (i.e., performed miracles, as was usual in those days) and beguiled and led Israel astray, that he mocked the words of the wise [the interpreters of the law who came to be regarded as authoritative]; that he expounded the scriptures in the same manner as the Pharisees; that he had five disciples; that he said he was not come to take aught away from the Law or to add to it; that he was hanged [crucified] as a false teacher and beguiler on the eve of Passover which happened on a Sabbath; that his disciples healed the sick in his name" (explanations in the brackets added by Kee).

The passages above testify to Jesus' existence as a historical figure and to some of the basic events of his life and those of his followers. But they tell us little else about the life or teachings of Jesus. Many people nowadays are distrustful of the canonical Gospels, preferring to believe that the truth about the 'historical Jesus' lies elsewhere. Type 'gospel' into Google, and the first 'gospel' to appear is the heretical and non-canonical Gospel of Thomas. It is unfortunate that this 'gospel' is searched more frequently on Google than the canonical Gospels because it is in fact much less historically accurate and reliable than the canonical Gospels themselves. The Gospel of Thomas, discovered in Egypt in 1945 and translated in 1977, consists of purported secret sayings of Jesus. It likely dates to the second century, much later than the canonical Gospels, and its themes are those that concerned second-century Gnostic heretics.

The Gnostics, as the Greek meaning of their name implies, were interested in 'secret knowledge' that leads to salvation, believed that spirit is good and matter is bad, and believed that sexual intercourse is evil since it is a function of the body, which is evil. For this reason, they altered Jesus' words about how his followers ought to become like children. It is no longer about childlike trust and humility as in the canonical Gospels, but about the child's lack of sexual development. In the Gospel of Thomas we read, "They said to Him, 'Shall we then, as children, enter the Kingdom?' Jesus said to them, '...when you make the male and the female one and the same, so that the male not be male nor the female female ... then will you enter [the Kingdom]'" (22).

There are a number of other, later Gnostic gospels. One is the 'Secret Gospel of Mark,' which is distinguished from the canonical Gospel of Mark. Some Gnostics, believing the body to be evil, believed that they could do anything they liked with the body; so while some shunned sexual intercourse, others indulged indiscriminately. According to this Gnostic text, the "mystery" of Christian initiation was to involve homosexual practices like those common with the pagan mystery cults. This, too, was not something that came from first-century Palestine or its interests or concerns, but was utterly foreign to it.

The 'Gospel of the Hebrews,' written in Greek but presumably having a Hebraic origin, opened with a strange explanation of Christ's coming: "When Christ wished to come upon the earth to men, the good Father summoned a mighty power in heaven, which was called Michael, and entrusted Christ to the care thereof. And the power came into the world and it was called Mary, and Christ was in her womb seven months" (1). St. Cyril of Jerusalem (ca. 313-386) in his *Discourse on Mary Theotokos* condemns this as heresy and instructs a monk to burn his copy of the Gospel of the Hebrews.

Other extracanonical 'gospels' have similar problems, and other early texts referring to the life of Christ that are cited by the Church Fathers only survive in small fragments. The Church and the bishops came to accept the four Gospels – Matthew, Mark, Luke, and John – as divinely inspired and suitable to be read in church. A student of St. Justin Martyr named Tatian sought to combine these four Gospels into a single flowing text. Even this the Church did not accept. Each canonical Gospel has its own flavor and purpose. The Church Fathers came to see the Four Gospels as representing divine purpose of the Gospel being proclaimed to the four corners of the earth and also came to associate each Gospel with one of the four living creatures in the Book of Revelation – the man, the lion, the ox, and the eagle (Rev. 4:6-8).

Reading the Canonical Gospels

We are left with canonical Gospels as the most historically reliable account of the words and deeds of Jesus. This is what the Church has always taught. According to the Second Vatican Council, the writers of the Four Gospels "told us the authentic truth about Jesus" (Dei Verbum, no. 19).

The Gospels are not intended as a chronology of the life of Jesus or as a biography in the modern sense. But biblical commentator Curtis Mitch proposes that they were indeed a biography in the ancient sense – that they are of the same genera as the classical Greek or Roman 'lives' (*bioi* or *vitae*), such as those written by Plutarch, Tacitus, Suetonius, and Philo of Alexandria. These ancient biographies were organized by set themes of the person's life, but expressed their real deeds and paraphrased what they really said, giving care to preserve the person's original intent. This is very much like the Gospels, in which each of the Gospels sets out on its own themes geared towards its intended readership yet incorporates many of the same stories about Jesus, though often with slightly different wording.

Each Gospel has its own purpose, theme, and flavor. For example, the Gospel of Matthew was written for Jewish Christians, contains many references to the Hebrew Scriptures, has the Kingdom of Heaven as its central theme, and gives us the image of Jesus the Messiah as the climax and fulfillment of the prophets and patriarchs of old. The Gospel of Mark, which explains Jewish customs to its audience, was written for Gentile Christians, most likely at Rome. This Gospel is concerned particularly with the issue of persecution and gives us the image of Jesus, the Son of God, as miracle-worker and exorcist. The Gospel of Luke, which is particularly concerned with the salvation of the Gentiles, was also written to a Gentile audience and it gives us a view to the personal touch of Jesus in his ministry. The Gospel of John presupposes that its readers are already familiar with the basic story and sets out by way of signs and discourses to inspire deeper faith in Jesus' divinity and his fulfillment of the Old Covenant.

Three of the Gospels – Matthew, Mark, and Luke – are very similar and share many of the same stories, even similar wording. These are called the 'Synoptic' Gospels since, in this way, they see Jesus as with 'one eye.'

Vatican II tells us of the writers of the Gospels, "Whether they relied on their own memory and recollections or on the testimony of those who 'from the beginning were eyewitnesses and witnesses of the word,' their purpose in writing was that we might know the 'truth' concerning the

things of which we have been informed" (Dei Verbum 19).
Scholars frequently point out that it seems the Gospel
writers were probably not recording the events from their
own memory since they often copied from one another. But
biblical scholar Richard Bauckham proposes that the
Gospels are indeed grounded in the reports of eyewitnesses.
He suggests in his book *Jesus and the Eyewitnesses* that the
numerous names of seemingly insignificant people, from
whose perspective many of the stories in the Gospels are
told, may indicate the sources for those stories. Also, Jesus'
mother Mary, who we are told in Luke 1:51 "kept all these
things in her heart," may have been an important
eyewitness. Curtis Mitch and Scott Hahn also propose the
Apostle Peter as a key eyewitness because stories from his
perspective have made their way into the Gospel of Mark,
and the man Mark is mentioned several times in the epistles
as one of Peter's collaborators in ministry.

Bauckham further proposes that many of the various,
seemingly insignificant figures mentioned in the Gospels
became members of early Christian communities, so they
were available to be consulted and could tell their stories to
other believers. As time went on and it became clear that the
end of the world was not as close as the early Christians may
have believed, Gospel writers, under the supervision of the

apostles, wrote down these stories to pass on to future believers and to bring faith to those who did not yet believe. Mark and Luke were not apostles themselves while Matthew and John were. Yet much debate remains about the identity of the actual writers of the Gospels and their connection to the names to which the Gospels were traditionally attributed.

The canonical Gospels set Jesus within the context of an externally verifiable history, but since dates were usually recorded in the years of the rulers and these political men had various governing roles over the course of their careers, the exact dating is a bit tricky. As we have already seen, the Gospel of Matthew tells us that Herod the Great, who historians tell us died in 4 BC, sought to kill the child Jesus out of fear for his kingdom. According to the Gospel of Luke, the event that brought Joseph and Mary to Bethlehem, where Jesus was born, was an enrollment by Caesar Augustus under Quirinius, the governor of Syria. But while both of these men belong to the historical record, neither a census by Caesar Augustus nor the term of Quiriunius as governor of Syria coincide with the rule of Herod the Great. Still, there are a few clues, as presented by Curtis Mitch and Scott Hahn. Josephus tells us that all Judea was required to swear allegiance to Caesar towards the end of the reign of

Herod the Great. Furthermore, it was customary for the Jews to return to the man's town of birth for such an enrollment. Also, Justin Martyr (d. 165) tells us that Quirinius, presumably a predecessor of Pontius Pilate, was 'procurator' of Judea before becoming governor of Syria. While history tells us that Quirinius became governor of Syria in AD 7, his prior post could explain his part in the enrollment.

According to the Gospel of Luke, Jesus was "about thirty years of age" at the start of his ministry (Lk. 3:23). If Jesus was born the same year that Herod the Great died (4 BC), that would bring us to the year AD 26 for the beginning of his ministry, plus or minus a few years. All four Gospels tell us that Jesus was baptized by John the Baptist just before his public ministry. The Gospel of Luke tells us that John the Baptist began his own ministry of preaching and baptizing "in the fifteenth year of Tiberius Caesar, when Pontius Pilate was governor of Judea" (Lk. 3:1). Tiberius became co-princeps of the Empire in AD 12 during Caesar Augustus' serious illness, but he fully became emperor in AD 14 after Augustus' death. From the first date, we could assume that John the Baptist began his ministry in AD 27, but from the second date, it would be AD 29. As for Pontius Pilate, his days as prefect of Judea (popularly called 'governor' or later 'procurator') extended from AD 26 to AD 36. Josephus also tells us about John the Baptist and that many of the Jews considered Herod Antipas' military defeat by Aretas IV of Nabatea, dated by scholars at AD 36, as a punishment from God for Herod's slaughter of John the Baptist. The Gospel of John records three separate Passover festivals during Jesus' ministry, so this would lead us to believe that Jesus' ministry extended at least through three such annual festivals. Since Pilate is the one who had Jesus executed and his term as prefect ended in AD 36, Jesus' ministry must have begun at least two or three years before that date. So from these historical facts, it seems that Jesus public ministry, as recorded in the canonical Gospels, began at some point between AD 27 and AD 34. But we can narrow it down further still.

At the first Passover mentioned in the Gospel of John, Jesus, standing in the Temple, prophesied, "Destroy this temple and in three days I will raise it up" (Jn. 2:19). The Jews retorted that the Temple had been under construction for 46 years. Josephus tells us that Herod began his renovation of the Temple in the eighteenth year of his reign, and we know that his reign began in 37 BC. Some say that Josephus may have been counting from the time Herod began working on the sanctuary itself, which was about two years into the project. So it would seem that the first Passover of Jesus' ministry fell between the year AD 27 and AD 29.

From all this, we can see that the Jesus of the canonical Gospels fits into the externally verifiable history of first-century Palestine.

The Human Origins of Jesus

Isaiah prophesied about the Messiah, "But a shoot shall sprout from the stump of Jesse [the father of David], and from his roots a bud shall blossom" (Is. 11:1). It seems that Jesus was of a more obscure branch of the line of David, yet he was truly Davidic unlike the rulers of the Hasmonean of Herodian dynasties. The famous biblical scholar Raymond Brown comments that had Jesus been a member of a more prominent Davidic line, there would have been much less controversy about his origins among his contemporaries.

The Gospel of Matthew and the Gospel of Luke both contain genealogies of Jesus. Many Davidic families maintained genealogies to preserve memory of their line. As mentioned earlier, Herod the Great had all such written genealogies that he could find destroyed to hide his own ignoble birth. It is possible that these Davidic genealogies provided a source for the ones found in Matthew and Luke. Many discrepancies exist between the two genealogies. Some of these discrepancies may be accounted for by gaps between the forefathers or by forefathers being known by multiple names. They both agree on his Davidic lineage and that the line passed through Zerubbabel, the great post-exilic governor of Judah under Persian rule.

The genealogy in Matthew doesn't shy away from mentioning, or even emphasizing, ancestors with unsavory pasts. The genealogies go through Joseph's line although Joseph was the foster father of Jesus, who was not conceived through the action of any man but by the Spirit of God. That Jesus was the adopted son of Joseph was not a problem since the adoption of a child was socially equivalent to having a natural-born child. Matthew mentions mothers in the line prior to Mary the mother of Jesus who didn't fit the mold: he listed Tamar, who schemed to conceive a child by pretending to be a prostitute; Rahab, the harlot at Jericho who hid the Israelite spies; Ruth, the pagan Moabite who adopted the faith of her Israelite husband Boaz; and Bathsheba, with whom King David had an adulterous affair before marrying her and begetting King Solomon. Perhaps Matthew was making the point that God writes straight with crooked lines, that Jesus took on a humanity tainted with sin in order to redeem it, or that he came even to save Gentiles. Biblical scholar Scott Hahn proposes that perhaps he was also comparing and contrasting Mary's virginal conception of Jesus with the way women in his line had conceived in the past.

We learn from the Gospel of Luke that Mary and Joseph lived in Nazareth, which was a very small village in Galilee. While today it is the most populous Christian center in Israel, it was probably inhabited by only a few hundred Jews at the time of Jesus, though it did have a synagogue as mentioned in the Gospels. No major roads passed through Nazareth, but the town was only five miles by foot from the much larger and more worldly-significant pagan city of Sepphoris, into which Herod the Great placed considerable pride and resources. The Gospels tell us in the Greek that Joseph, and hence his son Jesus, was a 'tekton,' which can be translated as either 'carpenter' or 'builder.' Some believe that Joseph laid bricks in the construction of buildings; others suggest that he crafted yokes for plowing. The Gospels speak of Jesus' brothers and sisters, but the term can also refer to cousins; and sacred tradition tells us that Mary was ever virgin.

Today, the grand modern Church of the Annunciation stands over a small cave, which is traditionally believed to be the structure for the home of Mary. Ancient, worn steps in the rock reveal a pathway in the small home, and now an altar stands in the grotto bearing the marvelous Latin inscription "Verbum Caro Hic Factum Est," which is translated "Here the Word Was Made Flesh." This may have been the site where the angel Gabriel announced God's plan for Mary to be the mother of Jesus and where she accepted that plan. Today there is also a living-history site called the Nazareth Village, in which visitors can experience what life must have been like in Jesus' time. A visitor will enter a small agrarian village with small stone houses and a stone well, from which veiled women in period dress draw water. There are also craftsmen at work, women tending to domestic affairs, children at play, shepherds tending to their flocks, and donkeys turning a turning millstone. The pace of life goes by very slowly there.

The angel told Mary, "The holy Spirit will come upon you, and the power of the Most High will overshadow you. Therefore the child to be born will be called holy, the Son of God" (Luke 1:35). Nazareth was small enough that people would begin to talk about a woman who was pregnant but not yet married, and there was no tolerance for such women. Virgins were typically given by their families in arranged marriages in their mid-teens, and the men were typically quite a few years older. The arrangement was sealed with a betrothal, which preceded the marriage by about a year. Both in Roman and Jewish society, the betrothal was legally binding, came with arrangements for a dowry, and, unlike a modern engagement, required divorce in order to break even though the couple did not yet live together. In case of divorce, the dowry had to be returned unless the woman was judged to be at fault. Premarital sex with another partner during a betrothal amounted to adultery, and the penalty for adultery under the Law of Moses was death by stoning. We read in the Gospel of Matthew, "Joseph her husband, since he was a righteous man, yet unwilling to expose her to shame, decided to divorce her quietly" (Mt. 1:19). Joseph would lose his right to the dowry with a quiet divorce; but first he would find that there was more to the situation than met the eye. Matthew continues, "Such was his intention when, behold, the angel of the Lord appeared to him in a dream and said, 'Joseph, son of David, do not be afraid to take Mary your wife into your home. For it is through the holy Spirit that this child has been conceived in her. She will bear a son and you are to name him Jesus, because he will save his people from their sins'" (Mt. 1:20-21).

The Birth of Jesus

But it was not in Nazareth that the Messiah was to be born. The prophet Micah foretold, "But you, Bethlehem-Ephrathaha least among the clans of Judah, From you shall come forth for me one who is to be ruler in Israel; Whose origin is from of old, from ancient times" (Micah 5:1). Luke tells us that it was the enrollment under Quirinius that brought Mary and Joseph to Bethlehem. Each man had to return to his native town to be enrolled, perhaps to swear an oath of allegiance to Caesar Augustus. Bethlehem, which literally means 'House of Bread,' was most famous for being the hometown of King David. Bethlehem is 70 miles south of Nazareth and four miles south of Jerusalem. Bethlehem was the town where Ruth and Boaz, ancestors of King David, met, married, and lived many centuries before. Only a few generations later, the prophet Samuel secretly anointed the shepherd boy David, the youngest son of Jesse, in the fields outside Bethlehem as king of Israel to follow Saul, who displeased the Lord. Outside the city are a number of large grassy fields spotted with bushes. King David used to tend his sheep in those fields as a boy. In Jesus' day, it was also a common place for shepherding and had a number of stone sheepfolds where the flocks could spend the night.

In the Letter to the Galatians we read, "But when the fullness of time had come, God sent his Son…" (Gal. 4:4). The fullness of time brings us from the Pax Romana to the side of the manger – a trough for feeding donkeys and oxen – in Bethlehem. We read of Mary in the Gospel of Luke, "While they were there, the time came for her to have her child, she gave birth to her firstborn son. She wrapped him in swaddling clothes and laid him in a manger, because there was no room for them in the inn" (Lk. 2:6-7). Pope Benedict XVI connects Jesus' makeshift place of birth to the maxim that Jesus later gives about his own ministry as a man: "Foxes have dens and birds of the sky have nests, but the Son of Man has nowhere to rest his head" (Mt. 8:20). As Pope Benedict also points out, the presence of this humble furnishing confirms the traditional image of Jesus being born in a stable.

Local Palestinian tradition as reported by Origen and Justin Martyr has Jesus born in a cave, so perhaps the stable was hewn out from a cave like many other structures in ancient Palestine. In fact, one of the Roman persecutions of Christians involved turning the cave, which had become a popular Christian pilgrim site, into a shrine for a pagan god. Today, the Church of the Nativity stands over the site. In the middle ages, Crusaders made the door to the Church of the Nativity very low to prevent raiders from storming into the church on horseback, as was common at that time in the

Holy Land. Thus, to this day, pilgrims must bend low to enter the place of Jesus' birth, recalling the Son of God who "emptied himself, taking the form of a slave" (Phil. 2:7). Pilgrims can also venerate the rock on which the manger may have lain. A silver star with an open center reveals the traditional spot.

Pilgrims today can visit Shepherds' Field, an expansive and sweeping plane covered in grassy vegetation and spotted with brush, which offers a view of the Bethlehem skyline in the background. Shepherds still tend their sheep there and make use of a number of stone sheepfolds. While kings were often spoken of as being 'shepherds' of their people, actual shepherds were not held in high regard and were often associated with low living and shifty dealings, as Raymond Brown points out. Yet it was to the shepherds that the angels first proclaimed the birth of Jesus in Bethlehem. An angel appeared to the shepherds in the fields proclaiming, "Do not be afraid; for behold, I proclaim to you good news of great joy that will be for all the people. For today in the city of David a savior has been born for you who is Messiah and Lord" (Lk. 2:10-11). The angel then described the place of Jesus' birth, and a chorus of angels sang out the famous words, "Glory to God in the highest and on earth peace to those on whom his favor rests" (Lk. 2:14). The shepherds went to visit the child and became the first outside his family to believe in Jesus as the Christ.

The Gospel of Luke tells us that Mary "gave birth to her firstborn son" (Lk. 2:7). 'Firstborn son' was a Jewish legal title that meant the child was the father's rightful heir and was required to be presented in the Temple forty days after his birth, as Luke likewise recounts. The term doesn't imply that the Virgin Mary bore any other children after Jesus. The presentation in the Temple was separate from the circumcision. Jewish boys were named and circumcised on the eighth day, and this event may also have taken place at the Temple, which was only a few miles away in Jerusalem. The visit to the Temple forty days after Jesus' birth was both for Jesus' presentation as firstborn and for Mary to take part in a ritual bath to remove the legal impurity that went along with giving birth to a boy. A sacrifice was required as part of this purification, and the family could only afford the poor person's offering – two turtledoves or pigeons. While at the Temple, the family came across the prophet Simeon and the prophetess Anna, who foretold marvelous and troubling things about the child and his mother. Simeon said to Mary, "Behold, this child is destined for the fall and rise of many in Israel, and to be a sign that will be contradicted (and you yourself a sword will pierce) so that the thoughts of many hearts may be revealed" (Lk. 2:34-35).

The Early Life of Jesus

We learn from the Gospel of Matthew about a star that led magi to Bethlehem. Fredrick Lawson, who conducted a recent popular study of the star of Bethlehem, used computer technology and biblical history to reconstruct the astronomy around the time of Jesus' birth. He believes that the star of Bethlehem was actually a cluster of stars, which came together to form a bright event in the sky about six months after the birth of Jesus and led the magi to Bethlehem to visit the child Jesus. Even the Gospel of Matthew tells us that the visit of the magi did not take place at the stable but rather at a "house" (Mt. 2:11).

'Magi' refers to a caste of Persian wise men. By the time of Jesus, the term came to refer more generally to oriental wise men believed to have access to superhuman knowledge. The magi in Matthew were probably astrologers familiar with the ancient belief that with a new king rises a new star in the heavens. Upon arriving in Jerusalem, they assumed that the new king was a son of Herod the Great, so they went first to see the king of Judea. But Herod became perplexed and assembled the chief priests, who cited the Scriptures to them that the Messiah was to arise from Bethlehem. As recalled earlier, this led to the massacre of innocents in Bethlehem by Herod, the holy family's flight into Egypt, and the return of the magi to their home by another route.

For Matthew, the story of the magi serves to show how Christ brings even the Gentiles to the Lord. It was prophesied in Isaiah: "Caravans of camels shall cover you, dromedaries of Midian and Ephah; All from Sheba shall come bearing gold and frankincense, and heralding the praises of the LORD" (Is. 60:6). Tradition came to attribute symbolic meaning to the gifts. Gold stood for Christ's kingship. Frankincense, a sweet-burning incense, stood for his high priesthood. Myrrh, a spice used in burial, was said to be used after his sacrificial death. Matthew does not tell us that there were three magi, only that there were three gifts of gold, frankincense, and myrrh. Tradition even gives us names for the magi and their countries of origin: Caspar from Tarsus in Asia Minor, Melchior from Arabia, and Balthazar from Ethiopia. The glorious cathedral in Cologne, Germany, even claims to enshrine the bones of the three magi, though there are a number of other churches throughout the world that make the same claim.

After the visit of the magi, Joseph was warned in a dream to flee to Egypt, a frequently used hideaway for those escaping Palestine, and thus avoided Herod's massacre of male infants in Bethlehem. The holy family's flight into Egypt and return to Palestine recall the exodus of the Hebrews out of Egypt by Moses, in which the people were freed from slavery. Remember that for Matthew, Jesus is the new Moses. Thus, Matthew quotes the prophet Hosea, who wrote, "out of Egypt I called my son" (Hos. 11:1). Upon learning of the death of the sick and elderly Herod the Great, Joseph brought the family back to Palestine. But he avoided Bethlehem, in the realm of the cruel ethnarch Herod Achelaus, and returned instead to Nazareth in the realm of Herod Antipas, who was a slightly less violent dictator.

Jews visited the Temple every year, at Passover, but we will not see another mention of such a journey in the Gospels until Jesus is twelve years old. According to the Jewish custom at the time, Jesus would have had his bar mitzvah by then, giving him adult responsibilities and duties as a Jewish man. This enabled him to sit with the scribes in the Temple and discuss the Torah with them at length. Meanwhile, his parents were making their way home with the caravan, assuming that Jesus was making the 65-mile trek with neighbors and family. But not finding him when the groups came together, they returned frantically to Jerusalem to search for him. After three days, foreshadowing Jesus' three days in the tomb, they found him in the Temple, probably in the colonnade enclosing the Temple Mount. Luke tells us that Jesus was "sitting in the midst of the teachers, listening to them and asking them questions, and all who heard him were astounded at his understanding and his answers" (Lk. 2:46-48). When his parents asked him why he had remained in the Temple, Jesus told them, "Did you not know that I must be in my Father's house?" (Lk. 2:49). First-century Jews did not casually call God their 'Father' as is common in our society today. Instead, Jesus, here at the age of twelve, was already articulating his own unique relationship with God.

Joseph, the foster father of Jesus, is not mentioned in the Gospel again except in reference to the past, as when townspeople recall that Jesus is the son of Joseph. So it is generally believed that Joseph, likely being older than Mary, died before Jesus began his public ministry. Meanwhile, Jesus probably remained inconspicuously working in or around Nazareth in his father's trade as 'tekton,' either as a carpenter or builder, and supported his mother Mary, who likely continued her domestic work. Jesus would have continued worshipping and hearing the Scriptures proclaimed at the synagogue in Nazareth with his neighbors and extended family, and he would have continued making routine pilgrimages to Jerusalem for the festivals. He seemed to the townspeople to be little different than the rest. The time of his manifestation had not yet come. The townspeople of Nazareth were not ready for it; in fact, they never would be.

The Emergence of John the Baptist

The great witness to Jesus as the Messiah was the prophet John the Baptist. In the Gospel of Luke, the births of John and Jesus are closely linked. As Pope Benedict writes, this is both to join them and to contrast them. Both births were announced by the angel Gabriel. Both children were conceived by God's power in humanly impossible circumstances: John was born to Elizabeth, a barren woman past childbearing age, and Jesus was born to a young virgin named Mary. Both were named by God through the angel rather than by their fathers – 'John' means 'God's gift,' and 'Jesus' means 'God saves.' Their mothers, Elizabeth and Mary, were cousins. John was born six months before Jesus, and he was to bear witness to Jesus and prepare his way. Both were declared holy to the Lord. But John's birth was announced by the angel to his father Zachariah, a priest serving in the Temple in Jerusalem, in one of its holiest and best-known chambers. Jesus' birth was announced by the angel to Mary, an unknown girl in the lesser-known town of Nazareth, in a humble and obscure family dwelling. Pope Benedict writes that this was to serve for us as an example of humility: the greater one is according to the spirit, the more humble he or she must be.

Zachariah, the father of John the Baptist, was "of the priestly division of Abijah" (Lk. 1:5). There were 24 priestly divisions, and each one served at the Temple for a rotation of two weeks each year. During that service, priests would be selected by lots to offer incense for the morning offering and for the evening offering in the Holy Place, which was the second-innermost chamber and thus the second holiest in the sanctuary. Priests typically received this privilege only once in their lifetime. The lots fell, one day, to Zachariah, who went in, offering prayers for the people and also his own supplication over his childlessness and the disgrace of barrenness that had fallen to his wife Elizabeth. We read in the Gospel of Luke, "Then, when the whole assembly of the people was praying outside at the hour of the incense offering, the angel of the Lord appeared to him, standing at the right of the altar of incense" (Lk. 1:10-11). The angel told Zachariah that he would have a son through Elizabeth and was to name him John. Zachariah did not believe the angel, so he was made mute until after the child's birth. At the child's naming, the relatives and neighbors were going to call him Zachariah after his father, but Elizabeth protested. They then went to Zachariah, who wrote on a tablet, "John is his name," at which his mouth was opened and he began to praise the Lord.

In the Temple, the angel had prophesied to Zachariah about John that "...he will be great in the sight of [the] Lord. He will drink neither wine nor strong drink. He will be filled with the holy Spirit even from his mother's womb, and he will turn many of the children of Israel to the Lord their God. He will go before him in the spirit and power of Elijah to turn the hearts of fathers toward children and the disobedient to the understanding of the righteous, to prepare a people fit for the Lord" (Lk. 1:15-17). The reference to his abstinence from wine indicated that he would be a 'nazirite,' a kind of Jewish ascetic who was 'set apart' for God, as the name implies. The book of Numbers says of this vow, "When men or women solemnly take the nazirite vow to dedicate themselves to the LORD, they shall abstain from wine and strong drink; they may neither drink wine vinegar, other vinegar, or any kind of grape juice, nor eat either fresh or dried grapes…. While they are under the nazirite vow, no razor shall touch their hair…. As long as they are nazirites, they are holy to the LORD. (Num. 4:2-3, 5, 8). Nazarites could take this vow either for a time or for their whole lives. For John, he was set apart in this way as long as he lived.

In the ninth century BC, the prophet Elijah stood up to King Ahaz, Queen Jezebel, and the priests of Baal to return Israel to the worship of the true God. The reference to Elijah in the angel's words about John the Baptist recalls the prophecy of Malachi: "Now I am sending to you Elijah the prophet, Before the day of the LORD comes, the great and terrible day; He will turn the heart of fathers to their sons, and the heart of sons to their fathers..." (Mal. 3:23-24). When the adult John the Baptist is described in the Gospel of Mark, we find that "John was clothed in camel's hair, with a leather belt around his waist. He fed on locusts and wild honey" (Mk. 1:6). This is how Elijah was described in 2 Kings: "He wore a hairy garment with a leather belt around his waist" (2 Kings 1:8).

We find in the Gospel of Luke that John the Baptist began his ministry of preaching and baptizing in the fifteenth year of the reign of Tiberius (Lk. 3:1). Depending on how the beginning of Tiberius' reign is calculated, this would be either AD 27 or AD 29. Baptism was a new practice, though rooted in the ancient Jewish practice of purification as required by the Law of Moses. Rituals involving purification by water were required after various bodily emissions, after sexual intercourse, after giving birth, after menstruation, and after death or touching a corpse. Oral tradition passed on by the rabbis also required purification before prayer, before meals, after excretion, and at many other occasions. Some scholars speculate that John the Baptist may have been influenced by or lived among the Essenes for a time since the Essenes greatly expanded the tradition of purification, even requiring daily baths of purification within the context of an ascetic life of self-denial similar to John's.

On the physical level, purification rituals promoted hygiene; but on a spiritual level, these rituals taught in a concrete fashion how God is holy and requires his people to be holy – and to be made holy through cleansing from sin. For this reason, Jesus taught, "It is not what enters one's mouth that defiles that person; but what comes out of the mouth is what defiles one" (Mt. 15:11). For John the Baptist, baptism was a sign of internalizing the cleansing physically required of Jews; it represented a commitment to internal holiness and to turning from the sin that defiles as the filth that defiles the body. According to Josephus, baptism for John followed the preaching on righteousness and the commitment of the person to turn from sin. He writes, "for that the washing [with water] would be acceptable to him, if they made use of it, not in order to the putting away [or the remission] of some sins [only], but for the purification of the body; supposing still that the soul was thoroughly purified beforehand by righteousness" (Ant. 15.5.2). The ancient Jews' general fear of mighty waters, as in the story of the Great Flood in which God wiped out all the earth, also played into the symbolism of baptism. Going down into the waters symbolized death, and rising out of the waters symbolized new life.

The baptism of John differed from the baptism that Jesus would bring, as John himself taught: "I am baptizing you with water, for repentance, but the one who is coming after me is mightier than I. I am not worthy to carry his sandals. He will baptize you with the holy Spirit and fire" (Mt. 3:11). John introduced elements of this new baptism that Jesus later brought. The baptism brought by Jesus actually effected what it symbolized – new life in Jesus bought by the power of Christ's death and resurrection. Of this new baptism Jesus taught, "no one can enter the kingdom of God without being born of water and Spirit" (Jn. 3:5).

John the Baptist and the Jews

John the Baptist's preaching was an event of great importance for the Jews of the time. The Gospel of Mark tells us, "People of the whole Judean countryside and all the inhabitants of Jerusalem were going out to him and were being baptized by him in the Jordan River as they acknowledged their sins" (Mk. 1:5). The Gospels tell us that these people included soldiers, tax collectors, religious leaders, and ordinary people, and that John provided strong moral exhortation for each group. Even Josephus, a Judeo-Roman historian who never became Christian, spoke of him in glowing terms and attributed much significance to his preaching. Josephus writes that John "was a good man, and commanded the Jews to exercise virtue, both as to righteousness towards one another, and piety towards God, and so to come to baptism" (Ant. 18.5.2). For the writers of the Gospels, the preaching of John the Baptist served as an important recommendation for the authenticity of Jesus' mission to those who did not yet believe.

The Gospels also show that John had great significance in God's plan of salvation as the messenger chosen to inaugurate the coming of the Messiah. All four Gospels cite the prophet Isaiah with reference to John the Baptist. Isaiah prophesied, "A voice proclaims: In the wilderness prepare the way of the LORD! Make straight in the wasteland a highway for our God! Every valley shall be lifted up, every mountain and hill made low; The rugged land shall be a plain, the rough country, a broad valley. Then the glory of the LORD shall be revealed, and all flesh shall see it together; for the mouth of the LORD has spoken" (Is. 40:3-5). The Gospels drew from the Greek Septuagint translation of the text, which implied that the voice itself was in the wilderness. These words pointed to John the Baptist, who not only called people into their inner wilderness of struggle against sin but also physically went out to the wilderness to preach.

The wilderness, the setting for the wandering in the desert, was a place of struggle against one's inner tendencies, away from one's comfort zone and distractions within the city or village. The wilderness into which John went was the desert between Jerusalem and the River Jordan. There were windswept mountains, sparse brush, extremely high temperatures during the day, and wild beasts such as gazelles, jackals, and lions. A pilgrimage from Jerusalem to see John the Baptist would entail a bit of hardship, and one can imagine the booming voice of the prophet echoing across the desert when they found him. The preaching led to baptism in the reed-lined waters of the River Jordan, waters once parted by God for Joshua's army to escape their enemies and enter the Promised Land.

Like Elijah, John the Baptist was unafraid of the rulers of his day. Herod Antipas divorced his wife, the daughter of Aretas of Nabatea, and took Herodias, the wife of his brother Philip the Tetrarch. He had become romantically involved with Herodias on a visit to Rome together with his brother Philip, and she consented to leave Philip and marry Herod. But in addition to being his brother's wife, Herodias was also his niece, making the union doubly illicit under Jewish religious law. John the Baptist spoke out against this illicit marriage, prompting Herod Antipas to arrest him and keep him prisoner, as Josephus tells us, at the fortress Machaerus, which is an austere and towering edifice in the desert region on the eastern banks of the Dead Sea.

Jesus was distressed over the arrest of John the Baptist and withdrew to Galilee after his own time away in the desert of Judea (Mt. 4:12). The imprisoned John, too, was concerned over Jesus, who had previously come to him for baptism. Perhaps John wanted further confirmation that he had indeed accomplished the task he believed God had sent him to do – to prepare the way for the Messiah. So he sent messengers to Jesus to ask, "Are you the one who is to come, or should we look for another?" (Mt. 11:3). The answer from Jesus came back, "the blind regain their sight, the lame walk, lepers are cleansed, the deaf hear, the dead are raised, and the poor have the good news proclaimed to them. And blessed is the one who takes no offense at me" (Mt. 11:5-6). Jesus did not give a direct response, but rather quoted this series of famous prophesies from Isaiah about the Messiah, showing that he in fact was fulfilling the deeds foretold of the Messiah.

It was at Herod's birthday celebration that John's fate was sealed. Herod was very much stirred by the erotic dance of Herodias' daughter Salome, his own great niece. He swore to give her anything she asked, up to half of his kingdom. The young adolescent asked her mother Herodias what to request, and she told her to ask for the head of John the Baptist on a platter. The Gospels tell us that while Herod was intrigued by John's sermons in the dungeon, he fulfilled the girl's request, and she gave the platter to her mother. Some time afterwards, Herod Antipas suffered a decisive military defeat at the hands of Aretas of Nabatea, a competing ruler and the father of his former wife. According to Josephus, the Jews widely attributed this defeat to God's judgment against him for the blood of John the Baptist.

Jesus' Baptism and His Temptation in the Desert

In prison, John would have remembered distinctly the crowning event of his career – baptizing Jesus, the Christ, in the River Jordan. One day as John went about his usual ministry of preaching and baptizing repentant sinners in the River Jordan, Jesus approached him for baptism. Matthew's Gospel tells us that John recognized Jesus as he approached. He did not want to baptize Jesus, recognizing his own sin and Jesus' superiority, and said to him, "I need to be baptized by you, and yet you are coming to me?" (Mt. 3:14).

John grew up in the village of Ein Karem in Judea, in the "hill country" not far from Jerusalem (Lk. 1:39). Jesus, his second cousin, grew up in Nazareth in Galilee about 65 miles to the north. From the Gospel of Luke, we find that Mary, after hearing from the angel the news of her own pregnancy and that of her older cousin Elizabeth, made the long trip south to tend to her cousin's needs before returning to Nazareth – only to have to return to Judea few months later with Joseph for the enrollment under Quirinius. At Ein Karem, the child John in his mother's womb stirred at the presence of Jesus in Mary's womb, and John's mother Elizabeth marveled at it and said to her younger cousin, "how does this happen to me, that the mother of my Lord should come to me?" (Lk. 1:43). The Gospels never tell us explicitly whether or not John and Jesus visited again before the event at the banks of the River Jordan, but it seems they would have at least seen each other occasionally at the yearly Passover pilgrimage to Jerusalem and that their mothers would have told their sons the marvelous stories of what God had done in their lives during their pregnancies.

John was right to question Jesus' need for baptism and to remark on his own need before Jesus. John's baptism was for sinners' repentance. Pope Benedict teaches that Jesus did not need the baptism for himself but to foreshadow what he would do on the cross for all sinners – die and rise again – and also to foreshadow the baptism that he would bring. So Jesus told John to proceed, saying, "Allow it now, for thus it is fitting for us to fulfill all righteousness" (Mt. 3:15). Pope Benedict tells us that 'righteousness' refers to living out the Torah, the Law of Moses. Jesus' baptism revealed in an obscure way his redemptive mission, which was the fulfillment of the Law of Moses. After the baptism, the heavens opened, a dove descended and rested on Jesus, and a voice from the heavens proclaimed, "This is my beloved Son, with whom I am well pleased." (Mt. 3:17). The image of the dove over the River Jordan recalls the Creation story from Genesis, in which the Spirit of God swept over the waters. It also recalls the dove that Noah sent out of the Ark after the Great Flood. The dove, sent out to find dry land, symbolized God's peace for the world after the Flood.

In the Gospel of John, John the Baptist recalls this event to the crowds saying, "I did not know him, but the one who sent me to baptize with water told me, 'On whomever you see the Spirit come down and remain, he is the one who will baptize with the holy Spirit'" (Jn. 1:33). According to St. Augustine, what John did not know about Jesus was that Jesus' new baptism that would be the ultimate baptism, which his own baptism prefigured. This was made clear to him by the Spirit's descent, marking the one who would baptize "with spirit and fire" (Mt. 3:11).

Jesus was baptized at "Bethany across the Jordan" (Jn. 1:28). The site – which differs from the Bethany in Judea, which was the home of Martha and Mary – is not known today with certainty, but it is believed to be on the banks of the Jordan just north of the Dead Sea. Pilgrims today can visit the possible spot on both the Israeli and Jordanian side of the River Jordan, which today serves as the border between the two countries. The golden dome of a Greek Orthodox church rises over the spot on the Jordanian side. The river there is rather narrow and murky today, lined by reeds and other vegetation, though it may have been wider and clearer in Jesus' day.

According to the Gospel of Mark, after Jesus' baptism, "At once the Spirit drove him out into the desert, and he remained in the desert for forty days, tempted by Satan" (Mk. 1:12-13). Jesus would have gone into the wilderness of Judea, which was not far from where John was preaching and baptizing. Only a few minutes by car from Bethany-beyond-the-Jordan through the scorching desert is the Mount of Temptation, just a short distance from Jericho in the wilderness of Judea in modern-day Israel. The area is barren, with only a few hardy bushes growing, and the earth there is covered mostly by rocks and sand. Perhaps this was the place to which the Devil took Jesus to give him a view of the kingdoms of the world, saying, "All these I shall give to you, if you will prostrate yourself and worship me" (Mt. 4:9). Jesus replied, "Get away, Satan! It is written; 'The Lord, your God, shall you worship and him alone shall you serve'" (Mt. 4:10). Christians would later remember Jesus' testing in the desert. The ascetic movement, which began in the late third and early fourth centuries, led some Christians who desired a more perfect life to go out into the desert to live like Christ, doing battle with the Devil and their own tendencies and devoting their time to prayer and meditation. These 'Desert

Fathers and Mothers' were the precursors of the monks and nuns.

There is much biblical symbolism behind the number forty, which was the number of days that Jesus fasted and prayed in the desert. For the Jewish mind, it recalled a time of trial and preparation. It was for forty years that the Children of Israel wandered in the desert before entering the Promised Land. During Jesus' forty days in the desert, he prepared himself for ministry by focusing on his relationship with the Father in prayer and by winning a victory in his battle with the Devil – as contrasted with the Children of Israel, who gave in so easily during their wanderings, worshipping the Golden Calf and grumbling against God and against Moses' leadership. It was also for forty days that the devastating rains continued during the Great Flood and for forty days that they subsided after the Ark came to rest on Mount Ararat. Interestingly, it was at the end of this latter forty days that Noah first sent out the dove to look for dry land (Gen. 7:6-8). The Gospel writers, painting for us the image of Christ and thinking in terms of theological symbolism, seem to have Noah in mind as a symbol of death and resurrection for all humanity.

The Call of the First Disciples

The Gospel of Mark tells us that Jesus began his ministry in Galilee after his temptation in the desert. But perhaps first Jesus returned to the nearby banks of the Jordan to the place of John's preaching. While the Gospel writers themselves were not much concerned with passing on a chronology of the events of Jesus' life, for our historical interests, it is worth noting that this would allow room for the account in John's Gospel that describes Jesus' first engagement of disciples of his own at the River Jordan after his baptism.

A devout Jew who had the liberty to do so could seek out a rabbi to become his disciple if the rabbi accepted him. The disciple was expected to submit to the rabbi and to adhere completely to his doctrines regarding God's Law, and thus learn to please God more fully. The scribes and Pharisees had disciples, as did John the Baptist. The Gospels speak of Jesus' followers as his disciples. But while disciples usually selected their own rabbi, the Rabbi Jesus was the one who selected his own disciples. Some disciples were called to follow him on the road wherever he went, though he possibly paused for a few months in the winter at Capernaum as N. T. Wright suggests. Others were simply called to accept and tend to the Kingdom of God within their hearts.

John the Baptist led some of his own disciples to Jesus. We learn in the Gospel of John, "The next day John was there again with two of his disciples, and as he watched Jesus walk by, he said, 'Behold, the Lamb of God'" (Jn. 1:35-36). John the Evangelist constructed his Gospel narrative around seven days in which the acts of Jesus reveal a new creation, similar to but surpassing the first one, which is also presented in terms of seven days. So it is possible that he did not mean that the event literally took place on the day after the baptism of Jesus but, rather, that it occurred after Jesus' temptation in the desert, which is recounted in the three Synoptic Gospels as immediately following the baptism.

In the presence of his disciples, John the Baptist called Jesus "the Lamb of God." Lambs were used for sacrifice, and only unblemished ones were considered fit for the purpose. Jesus was sinless, even though he received John's baptism for repentance, and God confirmed this fact through the voice from heaven: "This is my beloved Son, with whom I am well pleased." (Mt. 3:17). He would be the unblemished sacrifice that God would ultimately accept.

The Gospel of John tells us that after John the Baptist gave this testimony to Jesus, John's disciples Andrew and Simon, brother of Andrew, followed after Jesus. They were led to choose Jesus, it seems. But in the three Synoptic Gospels, it was at the shore of the Sea of Galilee that Andrew and Simon encountered Jesus; and in those accounts, it was Jesus who called them, and they immediately left their fishing boats, their father, and the hired help for their fishing business to follow him. Perhaps Andrew and Simon, fishermen by trade, were seekers of truth and disciples of John the Baptist who met Jesus first at the Jordan, but only followed him for a time. Perhaps they later returned to their father's fishing business, which was successful and stable enough to accommodate hired help, but then Jesus renewed and deepened their call to a more permanent discipleship as he made his way traveling and preaching throughout Palestine over the next three years. Or perhaps the various Gospel writers were more concerned with the spiritual significance of what happened in the call of Andrew and Simon than with the actual details of the events that surrounded it, as passed down by various oral accounts.

The Synoptic story of the call of Simon and Andrew, on the other hand, centers on the Sea of Galilee rather than the River Jordan. The Sea of Galilee, also called the Sea of Tiberias or the Lake of Gennesaret (which means 'harp'), is actually a freshwater body. Lined in part by palm trees and pebble beaches, and surrounded by rolling hills and grassy plains, the lake is 13 miles long, 8 miles wide, 144 feet deep, and sits about 700 feet below sea level. Today, pilgrims and tourists can still set out on sailboats on these mystical waters and take in the atmosphere. The cities that surrounded the lake hosted a great part of Jesus' ministry of preaching and healing. Jesus, in fact, took up residence in Capernaum on the north shore when he was not on the road. We learn from the Gospel of Mark, "When Jesus returned to Capernaum after some days, it became known that he was at home" (Mk. 2:1). It was in fact at this "home" that friends of a paralytic opened the thatched roof to lower the man down to Jesus when they could not make their way to him any other way because of the crowd.

The Sea of Galilee was a major center for fishing, with Josephus reporting it as hosting some 230 fishing boats. These wooden sailboats would have been about 30 feet long and sturdy enough to withstand both large catches of fish and the violent, sudden squalls that were common on the lake. Fishermen would fish at nighttime while tending to their boats and mending their nets, which would have been around 20 feet long, in the daytime. There were copious numbers of tilapia and other species of fish in the lake, and the fish caught would either be sold fresh at market or sent to be salted, packed in baskets, and exported to the far reaches of the Empire. Half of the men Jesus chose as apostles, his twelve core disciples, were Galilean fishermen. They were honest and hardworking men, but uneducated. Following this example, St. Paul would later write to the Corinthians church that he desires that "your faith might rest not on human wisdom but on the power of God" (1 Cor. 2:5).

One day, when a large crowd gathered to hear Jesus preach as he was leaving Capernaum for a preaching tour of Judea, he asked Simon for use of his fishing boat. Jesus saw that if he got into the boat and set out a bit, this would allow the people to see him better, give him some room to speak and gesture, and magnify his voice by way of the water. After the sermon, Jesus told Simon, "Put out into deep water and lower your nets for a catch" (Lk. 5:4). Simon grumbled a bit at this fishing advice coming from a carpenter-turned-preacher, but he gave it a try: "Master, we have worked hard all night and have caught nothing, but at your command, I will lower the nets" (Lk. 5:5). If they had caught little during the hours of the night, it would be even more unlikely that they would catch anything in daylight. But after he cast the nets, the nets sank low and began to tear, and the boat started to totter to the side under the weight of a huge catch of fish. Simon called to his partners' boat to come, but both boats together could hardly manage the load. When they had gotten back to shore and unloaded the fish, Simon said to Jesus, "Depart from me, Lord, for I am a sinful man" But Jesus replied, "Do not be afraid; from now on you will be catching men." Luke then reports, "When they brought their boats to the shore, they left everything and followed him" (Lk. 5:8-11).

While the Gospel of Mark does not tell us the role of the miraculous catch in the calling of Simon, it does mention that Jesus called Simon's brother Andrew from his fishing boat to come and follow him (Mk. 1:16). Mark also tells us that Jesus called James and John, the sons of Zebedee, while they were mending their nets in a boat (Mk. 1:19). Luke tells us that James and John were the partners of Simon who came to his rescue at the miraculous catch of fish.

We also learn from the Gospel of John that Jesus called Philip at Bethsaida, who immediately followed him, and that Philip in turn testified to Nathaniel about his belief in Jesus as the Messiah (Jn. 1:43-45). Nathaniel was at first skeptical because Jesus was from the insignificant Galilean town of Nazareth, but Jesus then gave Nathaniel a sign of his authenticity, saying, "Before Philip called you, I saw you under the fig tree" (Jn. 1:48). In this it seems that Jesus had read Nathaniel's thoughts and seen his concerns from afar about Jesus being the Messiah, since his reference is to Zechariah 3:10, which speaks of the coming of the Messiah: "On that day – oracle of the LORD of hosts – you will invite one another under your vines and fig trees." The once-skeptical Nathaniel's response was, "Rabbi, you are the Son of God, you are the King of Israel" (Jn. 1:49).

Proclaiming the Kingdom in Word and Deed

From the north shore of the Sea of Galilee, Jesus set out with his disciples – gathering more along the way – on three years of ministry on the road, proclaiming the coming of the 'Kingdom of God' and demonstrating it in action by healing people from sickness and casting out demons.

But first, according to the Gospel of John, Jesus and his disciples attended a wedding at Cana almost 20 miles to the southwest, in Galilee. It was five miles north of Nazareth, and Jesus' mother Mary was there. While the nuptials are not identified in the Gospel, some speculate that Mary may have been related to them since she was so concerned for their situation – the embarrassing predicament of running out of wine for the guests. Such a wedding celebration might last for days, and without wine, there would have been little with which to continue celebrating. Mary told the servers, "Do whatever he tells you" (Jn. 2:5). Looking at six stone jugs used for purification rituals, Jesus told them, "Fill the jars with water" and "Draw some out now and take it to the headwaiter." Such a request would certainly have seemed frivolous and possibly dangerous in front of their supervisor if nothing happened, yet the servers did just as he ordered. John reports, "So they took it. And when the headwaiter tasted the water that had become wine, without knowing where it came from (although the servers who had drawn the water knew), the headwaiter called the bridegroom and said to him, 'Everyone serves good wine first, and then when people have drunk freely, an inferior one; but you have kept the good wine until now" (Jn. 2:8-10). This was the first miracle we know of that Jesus performed publically. In drawing attention to himself, it was the beginning of danger from the religious authorities who would be watching him. Though hesitant to begin his public miracles, Jesus did so at a request from his mother for friends in need.

No early source disputes that Jesus truly worked miracles. Even Josephus, though probably not believing in Jesus' divine origin, still calls him "a doer of wonderful works" (Ant. 18.3.3). The canonical Gospels have differing but complementary perspectives on Jesus' miracles. For Mark, much emphasis is placed on Jesus' role as exorcist, scattering the forces of evil. In Luke, emphasis is placed on Jesus' actions of healing, showing his compassion for the suffering and disenfranchised. For Matthew, Jesus' healings are merciful acts that reveal the coming of the Kingdom of Heaven. For John, Jesus' wonders are arranged in a set of seven 'signs' that reveal the new creation brought by the Son of God. In fact, scholars call John 1:19-12:50 the 'Book of Signs,' with the changing of the water into wine as the first of the seven signs.

Both the miracles in the Synoptic Gospels and the signs in the Gospel of John are inseparable from Jesus' proclamation of the Kingdom. Pope Benedict writes that this proclamation "is not just informative speech, but performative speech…. God's word, which is at once word and deed, appears." According to the Gospel of Mark, "After John had been arrested, Jesus came to Galilee proclaiming the gospel of God" (Mk. 1:14). 'Gospel' literally means 'good news' and was a term used in the secular world for an official message from the emperor. Pope Benedict writes of the 'good news' ('evangelion' in Greek), "This term figures in the vocabulary of the Roman emperors, who understood themselves as lords, saviors, and redeemers of the world. The messages issued by the emperor were called in Latin evangelium, regardless of whether or not their content was particularly cheerful and pleasant. The idea was that what comes from the emperor is a saving message, that it is not just a piece of news, but a change of the world for the better."

To first-century Jewish ears, 'Kingdom of God' evoked images of the Kingdom of David and its coming restoration under the Messiah. Scott Hahn and Curtis Mitch call the Kingdom "God's sovereign rule over all nations through Jesus." Matthew's Gospel calls it the 'Kingdom of Heaven,' emphasizing its continuity with God's eternal realm. As to the nature of this Kingdom, Jesus would demonstrate it through parables, discourses, miracles, exorcisms, and signs. In one evocative parable, Jesus says of the Kingdom, "It is like a mustard seed that, when it is sown in the ground, is the smallest of all the seeds on the earth. But once it is sown, it springs up and becomes the largest of plants and puts forth large branches, so that the birds of the sky can dwell in its shade" (Mk. 4:31-32). After the resurrection, there is scant use of the term 'kingdom' in the New Testament since the word 'church' takes its place as the seed of the Gospel begins to sprout within the early Christian community.

Where the Kingdom is, evil is expelled. Thus, Jesus' preaching of the Kingdom in the Gospel of Mark begins with an exorcism. A man with an "unclean spirit" called out to Jesus while he was preaching in the synagogue at Capernaum. "Jesus rebuked him and said, 'Quiet! Come out of him!' And the unclean spirit convulsed him and with a loud cry came out of him. All were amazed and asked one another, 'Who is this? A new teaching with authority. He commands even the unclean spirits and they obey him" (Mk. 1:25-27). According to Hahn and Mitch, "While most exorcists of the day recited lengthy incantations or used odorous roots to expel demons, Jesus simply commands spirits and they leave." By his own power, evil was expelled in the wake of the Kingdom, and people were made whole as God intended them to be.

Another example of how Jesus proclaimed the Kingdom by powerful and divine action involves his interaction with people with leprosy. According to the Law of Moses, anyone with leprosy had to cry out, "Unclean, unclean!" (Lev. 13:45). Further, "As long as the infection is present, the person shall be unclean. Being unclean, that individual shall dwell apart, taking up residence outside the camp" (Lev. 13:46). Anyone who touched a person with leprosy likewise became unclean and in need of a laborious ritual-purification process. Meanwhile, a cured leper could be made ritually clean after making an offering, being examined by a priest, and being declared clean by him. We read in Leviticus, "The individual shall be brought to the priest, who is to go outside the camp. If the priest, upon inspection, finds that the scaly infection has healed in the afflicted person, he shall order that two live, clean birds, as well as some cedar wood, scarlet yarn, and hyssop be obtained for the one who is to be purified" (Lev. 14:3-4).

In Matthew's Gospel, however, we read, "And then a leper appeared and did him homage, and said, 'Lord, if you wish, you can make me clean.' He stretched out his hand, touched him, and said, 'I will do it. Be made clean.' His leprosy was cleansed immediately. Then Jesus said to him, 'See that you tell no one, but go show yourself to the priest, and offer the gift that Moses prescribed, that will be proof for them" (Mt. 8:2-4). While typically, when a Jew touched a leper, the former became ritually unclean, not only did Jesus not become unclean but the leprosy was also cleansed and the man was made clean. Jesus' order for the man to present himself to the priest was only because it would be "proof for them." The writer of the Gospel of Matthew is presenting us with an image of Jesus as above the Law of Moses and having the power to demonstrate it. This too means that "the kingdom of heaven is at hand" (Mt. 4:17) and that Christ comes with the power to make everyone spiritually clean before God through his touch. And it is only the "clean of heart" who will enter the Kingdom and ultimately "see God" (Mt. 5:8).

Itinerant Preacher

From the beginning of his ministry in Galilee, Jesus went about preaching, "This is the time of fulfillment. The kingdom of God is at hand. Repent, and believe in the gospel" (Mk. 1:15). Biblical scholar N. T. Wright writes, "The fact that Jesus was an itinerant prophet meant, clearly, that he went from village to village, saying substantially the same things wherever he went." For Wright, this accounts for some of the differences in the accounts of Jesus' sayings in the Synoptic Gospels when writing on the same teaching.

As we saw, Jesus called some of his disciples to leave everything behind and follow him wherever he went and to learn from him as rabbi. As Jesus went along, he passed by a toll collector sitting at a booth at Capernaum. Since fishing was Capernaum's largest trade, this much-hated toll collector would have inspected the daily catch and seized a generous portion for Herod Antipas and for himself. Jews were not to associate with Gentiles, but doing so was part of this man's daily work; and his job in fact required him to read and write in both Greek and Aramaic. He was considered low life. The man had a name – Matthew. And Jesus called him. In the Gospel of Matthew, we read, "He said to him, 'Follow me.' And he got up and followed him" (Mt. 9:9). It is astonishing that such a man would so easily follow an itinerant rabbi. The Pharisees, though, were not impressed at his change of heart, and they hated Jesus all the more for it. To them, it meant that Jesus was a friend of traitors to the pure Jewish religion, their way of life, and their desire for free nationhood. It is likely that this was among the first things that the Pharisees held against Jesus, and they would never let go.

Based on the three Passovers mentioned in the Gospel of John, and from piecing together Jesus' travels in relation to one another in the Synoptic Gospels, it is often surmised that Jesus went on three preaching tours of Galilee over the course of almost three years before he died, making excursions now and then. According to N. T. Wright, "We do not know for how many months in the year Jesus and his close followers were traveling, or whether, if they stayed in one place for the winter (as is not unreasonable to assume), that place would usually be Capernaum, where at least some of them had originated."

All four Gospels speak of Jesus' baptism by John in the River Jordan. After Jesus' temptation in the wilderness of Judea, he may have returned once more to the Jordan. Then, all of the Gospels agree, his first preaching took place in Galilee. From Galilee he moved on to Judea, where Jesus preached before going to the Temple for the first Passover of his public ministry. Already Jesus dangerously caused a stir, driving moneychangers out of the Temple and saying, "Take these out here, and stop making my Father's house a marketplace" (Jn. 2:16). Then Jesus and his disciples returned to Galilee but traveled through Samaria, even though it was customary for Jews to make a detour around the region since they despised its inhabitants for their mixed pagan-Jewish lineage and religious practices. Defying custom, Jesus held a spiritual discourse with a Samaritan woman at Jacob's well in Sychar and revealed his identity to her; she in turn brought her fellow villagers to belief (Jn. 4).

Each year, Jesus traveled around Galilee and then Judea, celebrating Passover at the Temple in Jerusalem. Then he would return to Galilee, making occasional excursions to outlying regions including Syrian-Phoenicia, Iturea, Trachonitis, the Decapolis, and Perea – ancient regions now within the modern-day borders of Lebanon, Syria, and Jordan. Jesus then made his final ascent into Judea for the Passover – a trip that would end with his arrest, passion, death, and resurrection.

Galilee was clearly the center of Jesus' ministry and travels. The Gospel of Mathew sees significance in the prophesy of Isaiah, who wrote, "Where once he degraded the land of

Zebulun and the land of Naphtali, now he has glorified the way of the Sea, the land across the Jordan, Galilee of the Nations. The people who walked in darkness have seen a great light; Upon those who lived in a land of gloom a light has shone" (Is. 8:23-9:1). These two tribes, towards the northern extreme of Palestine, had been long overrun by Gentiles. They were the first to be attacked by the Assyrians in 722 BC. Referred to as the "way of the Sea," the region was a crossroads for Gentile merchants and travelers between Egypt, Syria, and Persia. Even in the days of Herod the Great, who wanted to please his Romans overlords and Gentile subjects, Galilee was the chosen place for building pagan temples and pagan-styled cities. Farthest from the Temple, the center of Jewish life, Galilee was looked down upon by the Pharisees as a place of a looser and less precise interpretation of the Law of Moses and the tradition of the rabbis. They said against Jesus, "Look and see that no prophet arises from Galilee" (Jn. 7:52).

Yet it was Galilee that Jesus chose as his headquarters and to which he dedicated the lion's share of his efforts. Where better to preach God's 'good news' of redemption and restoration than to the poor and humble? As Jesus said elsewhere, "Those who are well do not need a physician, but the sick do. I did not come to call the righteous but sinners"

(Mk. 2:17). But Jesus came to call not only Jews but also Gentiles to accept the Gospel. Jesus said, "I say to you, many will come from the east and the west, and will recline with Abraham, Isaac, and Jacob at the banquet in the kingdom of heaven" (Mt. 8:11). Populated with cities mixed with Jews and Gentiles, and situated on the crossroads of the world, Galilee was an ideal location for preaching a message that was not for Jews alone but for all peoples.

Delivering the New Law

For the Gospel of Matthew, Jesus is the new Moses – that is, the new lawgiver. Jesus taught, "Do not think that I have come to abolish the law or the prophets. I have come not to abolish but to fulfill" (Mt. 5:17). Perhaps his most famous teaching is the Sermon on the Mount, found in Matthew's Gospel, which takes place within close view of the Sea of Galilee. Like Moses who went up a mountain to receive the Ten Commandments, Jesus "went up the mountain"; and like a Jewish rabbi teaching authoritatively, he "sat down" and gave eight prescriptions (Mt. 5:1). Luke's Gospel has the sermon taking place on a plain, with a different wording and arrangement. But as N. T. Wright points out that as an itinerant preacher, Jesus likely would have preached his sermons on many occasions to different audiences.

The Sermon on the Mount begins with Jesus' eight Beatitudes – eight blessings upon those who internalize and surpass the Law and have their citizenship not, primarily, in the earthly kingdom but in the Kingdom of Heaven. The great Hindu leader Mahatma Gandhi wrote in his autobiography of his own impression of Jesus' teaching, "...the New Testament produced a different impression, especially the Sermon on the Mount which went straight to my heart... That renunciation was the highest form of religion appealed to me greatly."

In contrast to the ambitious rulers of the day and to the self-complacent establishment, Jesus begins, "Blessed are the poor in spirit, for theirs in the kingdom of heaven" (Mt. 5:3). One might recall the Psalms: "The poor will eat their fill; those who seek the LORD will offer praise" (Ps. 22:27). Those who fear the Lord are lowly and detached from the goods of this world, regardless of their socio-economic status. Elsewhere the Psalmist wrote, "My soul rests in God alone, from whom comes my salvation" (Ps. 62:2).

Jesus continues, in contrast to those who are indifferent to the plight of the lowly and who turn a blind eye to the wickedness within themselves and society, "Blessed are they who mourn, for they will be comforted." Likewise the Psalmist wrote, "Why are you downcast, my soul; why do you groan within me? Wait for God, for I shall again praise him, my savior and my God" (Ps. 42:6).

Against the rage of kings and rulers and against the zealots who attempt to conquer by the sword, Jesus taught, "Blessed are the meek, for they will inherit the land." The Psalmist wrote, "But the meek shall possess the land, and delight themselves in abundant prosperity" (Ps. 37:11 [RSV]). The land is the Promised Land, and for Christians this finds its ultimate meaning in Heaven.

In contrast to those who are lukewarm or who only perform religious duties for appearances, Jesus proclaimed, "Blessed are they who hunger and thirst for righteousness, for they will be satisfied." In like manner, the Psalmist wrote, "For you my body yearns; for you my soul thirsts, In a land parched, lifeless, and without water" (Ps. 63:2). But the Psalmist wrote of the complacent, "They kill the widow and alien; the orphan they murder. They say, 'The LORD does not see; the God of Jacob takes no notice" (Ps. 94:6-7).

In contrast to the brutality of the Romans and the insensitivity of the Pharisees, Jesus taught, "Blessed are the merciful, for they will be shown mercy." The Psalmist wrote, "A clean heart create for me, God; renew within me a steadfast spirit.... I will teach the wicked your ways, that sinners may return to you" (Ps. 51:12, 15).

In contrast to those who only cleanse for ritual purification but are unconcerned about the filth within, Jesus preached, "Blessed are the clean of heart, for they will see God." The Psalmist wrote, "Who may go up the mountain of the LORD? The clean of hand and pure of heart, who has not given his soul to useless things, what is vain" (Ps. 24:3-4).

In contrast to those who live by the sword, Jesus taught, "Blessed are the peacemakers, for they will be called children of God." Likewise the Psalmist wrote, "Too long do I live among those who hate peace. When I speak of peace, they are for war" (Ps. 120:6-7).

Against those who hunt down others for challenging their complacent ways, Jesus said, "Blessed are they who are persecuted for the sake of righteousness, for theirs is the kingdom of heaven." The Psalmist wrote, "Why do the nations protest and the peoples conspire in vain? Kings on earth rise up and princes plot together against the LORD and against his anointed" (Ps. 2:2).

Continuing the sermon, Jesus told his hearers that not only must one refrain from adultery as the Law commanded, but one must also internalize that Law by refraining from lust; and he taught that not only must one not murder, but one must also internalize that Law by refraining from anger, hatred, and insults. He also taught, "You have heard that it was said, 'An eye for an eye and a tooth for a tooth.' But I say to you ... When someone strikes you on [your] right cheek, turn the other one to him as well" (Mt. 5:38-39). The Law of Moses was not condoning revenge but referring to the standard of proportionate justice that would be meted out lawfully to offenders. Moses said in Leviticus, "...eye for eye, tooth for tooth. The same injury that one gives another shall be inflicted in return … whoever takes a human life shall be put to death" (Lev. 24:20-21). But Jesus was calling for his followers not only to refrain from asking for more than is proportionate to an offense, but also to break the cycle of violence entirely by showing mercy in a remarkable way. Nor was he calling for passive victimhood, but rather, as commentator Fr. Robert Barron explains, Jesus preached non-violent resistance in standing one's ground.

On another occasion, Jesus was approached by a scribe who asked, "'Teacher, which commandment in the law is the greatest?'" He said to him, 'You shall love the Lord, your God, with all your heart, with all your soul, and with all your mind. This is the greatest and the first commandment. The second is like it: You shall love your neighbor as yourself. The whole law and the prophets depend on these two commandments" (Mt. 22:36-39). Here again Jesus spoke with a view to internalizing the Law; he revealed the heart of it all, which inspires the rest. Jesus was quoting the great Shema from Deuteronomy that every Jew would have learned since childhood to keep on their lips: "Hear, O Israel! The LORD is our God, the LORD alone! Therefore, you shall love the LORD, your God, with your whole heart, and with your whole being, and with your whole strength" (Deut. 6:4-5). He also added the love of neighbor, which is a principle that underlies much of the Law of Moses. Here, in a manner similar to the Rabbi Hillel, he quoted Leviticus, "Take no revenge and cherish no grudge against your own people. You shall love your neighbor as yourself" (Lev. 19:18).

The parallel account in Luke's Gospel tells us that the scribe, who likely felt silly receiving such a simple yet profound answer that every Jew ought to know, wanted to justify himself. So he asked, "And who is my neighbor?" (Lk. 10:29). This question elicited the famous parable of the Good Samaritan in which Jesus expanded the understanding of 'neighbor' to include all of humanity, thus broadening the command to love so that it encompassed Gentiles, enemies, and unbelievers.

Parables were one of Jesus' preferred forms of teaching. He would not answer a question directly but would instead tell a story with an unexpected twist, using familiar images, in which the hearer would have to enter the narrative and draw his or her own conclusion. In the parable of the Good Samaritan, a man falls prey to robbers on the perilous road to Jericho and is left for dead by a priest and a Levite, who do not want the hassle of becoming ritually unclean by touching the man. Only a Samaritan – and the Jews thought very little of Samaritans – showed mercy to the man, even going to great lengths to see to his safety and recovery. The scribe was forced to answer, after hearing the parable, that the Samaritan, too, was 'neighbor.'

In fact, few surviving texts of parables compare with Jesus' own style despite the existence of similar pedagogical methods in both Hebrew and Greek antiquity. One might think, for example, of Aesop's fables. Aesop told the story of a dog with a piece of meat in his mouth who saw his own reflection while crossing a bridge. The dog thought he was seeing another dog with a bigger piece of meat, so he lunged at the other dog in the river below and opened his mouth in a growl – only to lose the piece of meat and be swept away by the current. In a fable like this, unlike Jesus' parables, the characters are personified animals, and there is no reference to the hearer.

Parables are mentioned in the Old Testament, often as short, cryptic sayings, but they, too, differ significantly from Jesus' parables. The parable that is perhaps closest to the style used by Jesus is the one that the prophet Nathan told to King David. David had lusted after Bathsheba, the wife of Uriah, and committed adultery with her, fathering a child. After a failed attempt to cover up his crime, David had Uriah moved to the front lines of the battle with the Philistines, where he was killed in battle. So Nathan approached the king with a parable: there was a poor man who had only one ewe, whom he loved very much; but one day a rich man who had many ewes slaughtered and ate it. He then asked the king what should be done with that man. The king became enraged and declared that the man must die. Nathan responded, "You are the man!" (2 Sam. 12:7). It is possible that rabbis in Jesus' day used similar parables.

Jesus' parables are marked by their special relationship between the teacher and the hearer, who is not allowed to remain passive but must actively enter and complete the parable for himself. Professor David Gowler writes of Jesus' parables, "Communication in parable does not allow a passive role; the interlocutor participates in the formation of meaning as do, broadly speaking, the whole complex of social situations in which the utterance occurred. Parable can never be understood or explained outside of the link to the concrete situations of both the creator and hearer/reader." Gowler continues, "Jesus created them with one ear already attuned to our answers. Parables, therefore, are profoundly dialogic and do not pretend to be the last word because, in parable, the last word is continually granted to others...."

Conclusion

The story of Jesus does not stop here, of course. In fact, the story of Jesus will not even stop at the end of this series, which will conclude in the next volume with Jesus' resurrection and its profound effects on the first believers. The story of Jesus is a story that involves each member of the human race and, particularly, the whole people of God, who are called the Church.

Jesus belonged to a story to begin with – the story of God's intervention in the history of the Chosen People. As God, Jesus was also the Author of the story into which he entered. It was a story of high priests, prophets, and kings, and when Christ emerged, Israel was suffering a lack of leadership and continuity in all of those areas because of sin. Herod the Great brutally ruled Palestine under Rome. High priests were chosen by Herod without regard for proper lineage aside from being of the tribe of Levi. The Pharisees provided religious leadership but, as Jesus accused, led people astray by focusing on externals rather than on the heart of the Law. Furthermore, the Temple, though gloriously reconstructed by Herod, was nonetheless in a sorry state because the Holy of Holies was completely empty since the Ark of the Covenant had been lost centuries beforehand.

Jesus came to bring healing to this history, fulfillment of the Law and the prophets, and redemption from sin for the human race. He was not the only one claiming to be the Messiah, but he was the only Messiah-claimant to have a thriving movement a few years after his death, let alone two thousand years later. Ultimately, Christians would gain control of the Empire that crucified Christ, and the story would go on. Jesus was also unique as a Messiah-claimant to have a forerunner independent from himself, arranged by God's Providence – namely John the Baptist. John introduced the practice and symbolism of baptism as an internalization of the purification rituals of the Jews; and Jesus made use of it as the initiation for his followers, bringing with it his saving power. Already, in fact, baptism foreshadowed Christ's death and resurrection, into which his followers, too, must enter.

Jesus also belongs solidly to the externally verifiable historical record, as do the canonical Gospels. Both Roman and Jewish sources of the time reference Jesus in a manner that is consistent with what we learn of him from the canonical Gospels. Also, the apocryphal gospels have shown themselves to be less historically accurate than the canonical ones that the Church preserved and handed on. Those apocryphal gospels belie heretical interests, which emerged only generations after Jesus' time and often perverted his message. The canonical Gospels, on the other hand, each provide a different but generally complementary perspective on Christ. They were each written within a generation of Jesus, included stories that were passed orally through the Christian community, and were arranged primarily with theological ends in view while preserving the truth of what Jesus actually said and did.

Emerging from his baptism by John and his temptation in the desert, Jesus selected disciples for himself, even though typically disciples chose their rabbi. Preferring the humble, honest, but uneducated, he chose several Galilean fishermen; and choosing the contrite, he selected a tax collector. He also selected Galilee for the center of his ministry, preaching redemption to the lost and hope for the Gentiles. Jesus hit the road with his disciples for the next three years, going about proclaiming the coming of God's Kingdom with both words and powerful deeds. This kingdom was the Kingdom of David, come in a mysterious way that bubbled up to eternal life. By his exorcisms, he showed that in the Kingdom evil is expelled. By his healings, he showed that in the Kingdom all will be whole. And by his signs, he revealed himself to be the true Messiah and, further, to be God's only begotten Son.

Those who had citizenship in this Kingdom were not merely those who had lineage to Abraham, but those who practiced his Beatitudes and his New Law, which internalized and universalized the Law of Moses. To inculcate the morality of the Kingdom, he made creative use of parables that engaged his hearers and elicited a response from them.

Not all would respond. Even from the beginning of his ministry, the signs of his approaching passion and death were present. Jesus overturned the moneychangers' tables in the Temple at the first Passover of his public ministry. He chose Matthew, a tax collector who was perceived by the Pharisees as a traitor, as a disciple and later an apostle. Standing above the Law with power, he would touch lepers and make them clean, whereas according to the Law, anyone who touches a leper becomes himself unclean. And this was only the beginning. From the start, Jesus did not shy away from controversy, knowing that as John the Baptist prophesied, he was the "Lamb of God" to be offered as a fitting sacrifice for the people.

As C. S. Lewis wrote of Aslan, who represents Christ in *The Chronicles of Narnia*, "'Course he's not safe! But he's good."

To be continued...

Please enjoy the first two chapters of Pope Francis: Pastor of Mercy, also written by Michael J. Ruszala, as available from Wyatt North Publishing.

Pope Francis: Pastor of Mercy

Chapter 1

There is something about Pope Francis that captivates and delights people, even people who hardly know anything about him. He was elected in only two days of the conclave, yet many who tried their hand at speculating on who the next pope might be barely included him on their lists. The evening of Wednesday, March 13, 2013, the traditional white smoke poured out from the chimney of the Sistine Chapel and spread throughout the world by way of television, Internet, radio, and social media, signaling the beginning of a new papacy.

As the light of day waned from the Eternal City, some 150,000 people gathered watching intently for any movement behind the curtained door to the loggia of St. Peter's. A little after 8:00 p.m., the doors swung open and Cardinal Tauran emerged to pronounce the traditional and joyous Latin formula to introduce the new Bishop of Rome: "Annuncio vobis gaudium magnum; habemus papam!" ("I announce to you a great joy: we have a pope!") He then announced the new Holy Father's identity: "Cardinalem Bergoglio..."

The name Bergoglio, stirred up confusion among most of the faithful who flooded the square that were even more clueless than the television announcers were, who scrambled to figure out who exactly the new pope was. Pausing briefly, Cardinal Tauran continued by announcing the name of the new pope: "...qui sibi nomen imposuit Franciscum" ("who takes for himself the name Francis"). Whoever this man may be, his name choice resonated with all, and the crowd erupted with jubilant cheers. A few moments passed before the television announcers and their support teams informed their global audiences that the man who was about to walk onto the loggia dressed in white was Cardinal Jorge Mario Bergoglio, age 76, of Buenos Aires, Argentina.

To add to the bewilderment and kindling curiosity, when the new pope stepped out to the thunderous applause of the crowd in St. Peter's Square, he did not give the expected papal gesture of outstretched arms. Instead, he gave only a simple and modest wave. Also, before giving his first apostolic blessing, he bowed asking the faithful, from the least to the greatest, to silently pray for him. These acts were only the beginning of many more words and gestures, such as taking a seat on the bus with the cardinals, refusing a popemobile with bulletproof glass, and paying his own hotel bill after his election, that would raise eyebrows among some familiar with papal customs and delight the masses.

Is he making a pointed critique of previous pontificates? Is he simply posturing a persona to the world at large to make a point? The study of the life of Jorge Mario Bergoglio gives a clear answer, and the answer is no. This is simply who he is as a man and as a priest. The example of his thought-provoking gestures flows from his character, his life experiences, his religious vocation, and his spirituality. This book uncovers the life of the 266th Bishop of Rome, Jorge Mario Bergoglio, also known as Father Jorge, a name he preferred even while he was an archbishop and cardinal.

What exactly do people find so attractive about Pope Francis? Aldo Cagnoli, a layman who developed a friendship with the Pope when he was serving as a cardinal, shares the following: "The greatness of the man, in my humble opinion lies not in building walls or seeking refuge behind his wisdom and office, but rather in dealing with everyone judiciously, respectfully, and with humility, being willing to learn at any moment of life; that is what Father Bergoglio means to me" (as quoted in Ch. 12 of Pope Francis: Conversations with Jorge Bergoglio, previously published as El Jesuita [The Jesuit]).

At World Youth Day 2013, in Rio de Janeiro, Brazil, three million young people came out to celebrate their faith with Pope Francis. Doug Barry, from EWTN's Life on the Rock, interviewed youth at the event on what features stood out to them about Pope Francis. The young people seemed most touched by his authenticity. One young woman from St. Louis said, "He really knows his audience. He doesn't just say things to say things... And he is really sincere and genuine in all that he does." A friend agreed: "He was looking out into the crowd and it felt like he was looking at each one of us...." A young man from Canada weighed in: "You can actually relate to [him]... for example, last night he was talking about the World Cup and athletes." A young woman added, "I feel he means what he says... he practices what he preaches... he states that he's there for the poor and he actually means it."

The Holy Spirit guided the College of Cardinals in its election of Pope Francis to meet the needs of the Church following the historic resignation of Pope Benedict XVI due to old age. Representing the growth and demographic shift in the Church throughout the world and especially in the Southern Hemisphere, Pope Francis is the first non-European pope in almost 1,300 years. He is also the first Jesuit pope. Pope Francis comes with a different background and set of experiences. Both as archbishop and as pope, his flock knows him for his humility, ascetic frugality in solidarity with the poor, and closeness. He was born in Buenos Aires to a family of Italian immigrants, earned a diploma in chemistry, and followed a priestly vocation in the Jesuit order after an experience of God's mercy while receiving the sacrament of Reconciliation. Even though he is known for his smile and humor, the world also recognizes Pope Francis as a stern figure that stands against the evils of the world and challenges powerful government officials, when necessary.

The Church he leads is one that has been burdened in the West by the aftermath of sex abuse scandals and increased secularism. It is also a Church that is experiencing shifting in numbers out of the West and is being challenged with religious persecution in the Middle East, Asia, and Africa.

The Vatican that Pope Francis has inherited is plagued by cronyism and scandal. This Holy Father knows, however, that his job is not merely about numbers, politics, or even success. He steers clear of pessimism knowing that he is the head of Christ's Body on earth and works with Christ's grace. This is the man God has chosen in these times to lead his flock.

Chapter 2: Early Life in Argentina

Jorge Mario Bergoglio was born on December 17, 1936, in the Flores district of Buenos Aires. The district was a countryside locale outside the main city during the nineteenth century and many rich people in its early days called this place home. By the time Jorge was born, Flores was incorporated into the city of Buenos Aires and became a middle class neighborhood. Flores is also the home of the beautiful Romantic-styled Basilica of San José de Flores, built in 1831, with its dome over the altar, spire over the entrance, and columns at its facade. It was the Bergoglios' parish church and had much significance in Jorge's life.

Jorge's father's family had arrived in Argentina in 1929, immigrating from Piedimonte in northern Italy. They were not the only ones immigrating to the country. In the late nineteenth century, Argentina became industrialized and the government promoted immigration from Europe. During that time, the land prospered and Buenos Aires earned the moniker "Paris of the South." In the late nineteenth and early twentieth centuries waves of immigrants from Italy, Spain, and other European countries came off ships in the port of Buenos Aires. Three of Jorge's great uncles were the first in the family to immigrate to Argentina in 1922 searching for better employment opportunities after World War I. They established a paving company in Buenos Aires and built a four-story building for their company with the city's first elevator. Jorge's father and paternal grandparents followed the brothers in order to keep the family together and to escape Mussolini's fascist regime in Italy. Jorge's father and grandfather also helped with the business for a time. His father, Mario, who had been an accountant for a rail company in Italy, provided similar services for the family business (Cardinal Bergoglio recalls more on the story of his family's immigration and his early life in Ch. 1 of Conversations with Jorge Bergoglio).

Providentially, the Bergoglios were long delayed in liquidating their assets in Italy; this forced them to miss the ship they planned to sail on, the doomed Pricipessa Mafalda, which sank off the northern coast of Brazil before reaching Buenos Aires. The family took the Giulio Cesare instead and arrived safely in Argentina with Jorge's Grandma Rosa. Grandma Rosa wore a fur coat stuffed with the money the family brought with them from Italy. Economic hard times eventually hit Argentina in 1932 and the family's paving business went under, but the Bergoglio brothers began anew.

Jorge's father, Mario, met his mother Regina at Mass in 1934. Regina was born in Argentina, but her parents were also Italian immigrants. Mario and Regina married the following year after meeting. Jorge, the eldest of their five children, was born in 1936. Jorge fondly recalls his mother gathering the children around the radio on Sunday afternoons to listen to opera and explain the story. A true porteño, as the inhabitants of the port city of Buenos Aires are called, Jorge liked to play soccer, listen to Latin music, and dance the tango. Jorge's paternal grandparents lived around the corner from his home. He greatly admired his Grandma Rosa, and keeps her written prayer for her grandchildren with him until this day. Jorge recalls that while his grandparents kept their personal conversations in Piedmontese, Mario chose mostly to speak Spanish, preferring to look forward rather than back. Still, Jorge grew up speaking both Italian and Spanish.

Upon entering secondary school at the age of thirteen, his father insisted that Jorge begin work even though the family, in their modest lifestyle, was not particularly in need of extra income. Mario Bergoglio wanted to teach the boy the value of work and found several jobs for him during his adolescent years. Jorge worked in a hosiery factory for several years as a cleaner and at a desk. When he entered technical school to study food chemistry, Jorge found a job working in a laboratory. He worked under a woman who always challenged him to do his work thoroughly. He remembers her, though, with both fondness and sorrow. Years later, she was kidnapped and murdered along with members of her family because of her political views during the Dirty War, a conflict in the 1970's and 80's between the military dictatorship and guerrilla fighters in which thousands of Argentineans disappeared.

Initially unhappy with his father's decision to make him work, Jorge recalls later in his life that work was a valuable formative experience for him that taught him responsibility, realism, and how the world operated. He learned that a person's self worth often comes from their work, which led him to become committed later in life to promote a just culture of work rather than simply encouraging charity or entitlement. He believes that people need meaningful work in order to thrive. During his boyhood through his priestly ministry, he experienced the gulf in Argentina between the poor and the well off, which left the poor having few opportunities for gainful employment.

At the age of twenty-one, Jorge became dangerously ill. He was diagnosed with severe pneumonia and cysts. Part of his upper right lung was removed, and each day Jorge endured the pain and discomfort of saline fluid pumped through his chest to clear his system. Jorge remembers that the only person that was able to comfort him during this time was a religious sister who had catechized him from childhood, Sister Dolores. She exposed him to the true meaning of suffering with this simple statement: "You are imitating Christ." This stuck with him, and his sufferings during that time served as a crucible for his character, teaching him how to distinguish what is important in life from what is not. He was being prepared for what God was calling him to do in life, his vocation.

45116240R00088

Made in the USA
San Bernardino, CA
01 February 2017